• HALSGROVE DISCOVER SERIES ➤

THE
WHERRYMAN'S WAY

A GUIDE TO NORFOLK'S LONG DISTANCE FOOTPATH

STEVE SILK

HALSGROVE

First published in Great Britain in 2010

British Library Cataloguing-in-Publication Data
A CIP record for this title is available from the British Library

ISBN 978 1 84114 852 6

HALSGROVE
Halsgrove House,
Ryelands Industrial Estate,
Bagley Road, Wellington, Somerset TA21 9PZ
Tel: 01823 653777   Fax: 01823 216796
email: sales@halsgrove.com

Part of the Halsgrove group of companies
Information on all Halsgrove titles is available at: www.halsgrove.com

Printed and bound in China by Toppan Leefung Printing Ltd

*This book is dedicated to Debbie, Abbie and Maya.
Yes, we can go for a walk somewhere else now.*

Contents

The Wherryman's Way

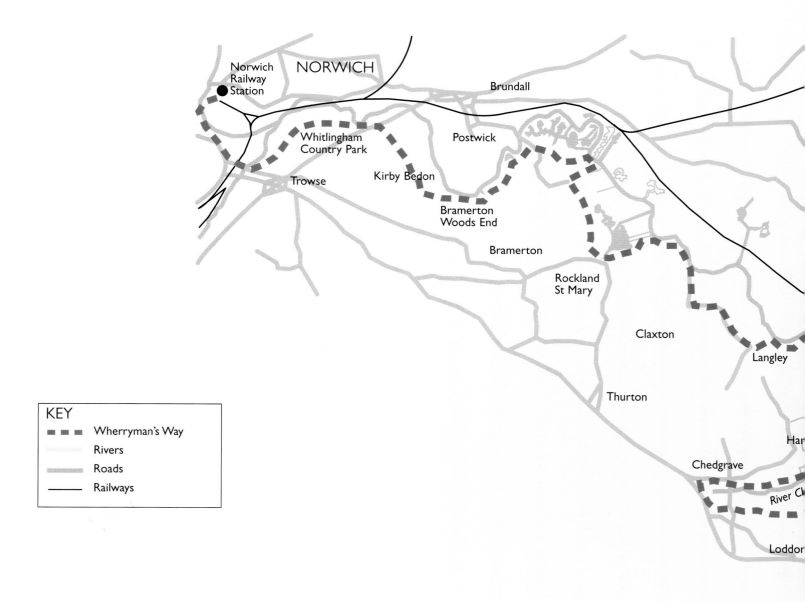

KEY

- ▬ ▬ ▬ Wherryman's Way
- Rivers
- Roads
- Railways

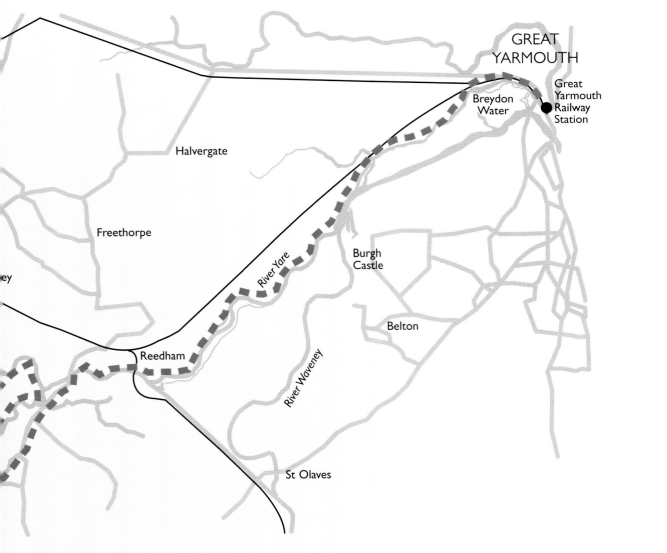

GREAT
YARMOUTH

Great
Yarmouth
Railway
Station

Breydon
Water

Halvergate

Freethorpe

River Yare

Burgh
Castle

Belton

River Waveney

Reedham

St Olaves

THANKS TO...

The many helpful and patient staff at the Norfolk and Norwich Millennium Library and also at Loddon Library.

Also, starting upstream and heading down river: Guy Cooper, Lesley Owen-Edwards, Jane Flatt, John Renton, Mike Sparkes, Andy Cullum, Roger Mayhew, Janet Smith, Vaughan Ashby, Norwich Frostbites, Chris Fisher, Clive Rainbird, Brian Anwell, Ted Cullum, Richard Crosskill, Mark Wells, Phil Reeve, Millie Reeve, Colin Barnes, John Ellis, Mary Upton, Alan Mallett, Tim Strudwick, Geoff Pinder, Aidan Ward, Simon Cullum and Buckenham Sailing Club, Peter White, Paul and Myrtle Wright, John Scott, Raz Woollacott, Tony Timmins, Bill Carson, Richard Rockley, Cecil Nicholls, Freda Selby, Anthony Ward, Carol Carpenter, Christina Crease, Sarah Scott, Caroline Dwen, Roger Kidner, Dennis Walklin, Fiona and Richard Husband, Frances and Aidan Kirkpatrick, Eric Wilkinson, David Dicks, Caroline Milton, Jonathan Greenway, Paul Parravani, Andy and Katherine Walter, Mike Saunders, Tricia Betts, Pamela Blinkhorn, Dr Barbara Linsley, Graham Carlton, Colin Sanderson, Alison Yardy, Sheila and Paul Hutchinson, Tony Webster, The Rev Damon Rogers, David Archer, Stephen Williamson, Robert and Annette Terry, Bill and Ros Carter, John Orsbourn, John Ralph and Tracy Bold, Barry Brooks, Mark Smart, Jack Harrison, Margaret Dunnett, Richard Burnett, Steve "Tug" Wilson, Norma Watt, Stephanie Gowman, Jonathan Neville, and of course Simon Butler from Halsgrove.

Barbara Miller, Jane Flatt, Chris Fisher, Tony Parker, Mark Cocker, Christina Crease, Carol Carpenter, Sheila and Paul Hutchinson, Stephen Williamson and Colin Tooke helped enormously with their expertise on particular chapters while the skipper and crew of the *Limon* provided a whole different perspective.

Thanks also to Norfolk County Council for permission to use the Wherryman's Way logo.

Not forgetting Mum, Dad and Caroline for their constant encouragement, Caroline for her invaluable proof-reading skills and Martin despite the fact he'll never make it this far.

Photo credits

Many thanks to all of the following for permission to use their photos: particularly Mike Page for his aerial shots:

Page 7 Wherry: Mike Page; Page 8 Wherry: Picture Norfolk; Page 9 Albion: from Mike Sparkes's collection; Page 13 Steam Packet: Picture Norfolk; Page 16 Colman's pictures: reproduced by permission of Unilever from originals held in the Unilever Archives; Page 22 both pictures from Mike Sparkes's collection; Page 24 Whitlingham aerial: Mike Page; Page 27 White House: Picture Norfolk; Page 29 Chalk pit: Picture Norfolk; Page 30 Nobby Clarke via Andy Cullum; Page 32 Billy Bluelight: Archant; Page 36 Mark Wells: Philip Leftley; Page 41 The Ferry House: Roger Hales; Page 43 Dr Joyce Lambert: Archant; Page 47 Ted Ellis: via John Ellis; Page 53 Rockland aerial: Mike Page; Page 61 Farmer Pyke: via Chris Fisher; Page 76 Mill sketch: Anthony Ward; Page 76 Dusk at Cantley: Simon Wright; Page 78 The cap goes on: Richard Rockley; Page 79 Staithe archive: Picture Norfolk; Page 80 Hardley Cross archive: Picture Norfolk; Pages 88&89 Archive: Loddon Local History Archive; Page 105 Mike Saunders: Archant; Page 110 Reedham Ferry Aerial: Mike Page; Page 124 Breydon Aerial: Mike Page; Page 130 Sheila Hutchinson; Page 132 Breydon Wherry via Mike Sparkes; Page 136 Yarmouth aerial: Mike Page; Page 139 Church archive: Picture Norfolk; Page 140 Lower Ferry: Jack Harrison

Introduction

About ten miles north of the Wherryman's Way lies a boatshed on a short dyke known as Womack Water.

Protected from the elements, two ancient boats lie side by side. They are *Maud* and *Albion*, the only surviving trading wherries in the world. A century ago wherries were the heavy goods vehicles of their day, carrying vast cargoes right across the Broads network. Those days are long gone, but if it wasn't for these two grand old ladies, they might be forgotten too.

While *Maud* and *Albion* are based just off the River Thurne, the wherry's heartland was the River Yare. The Yare combines with a short stretch of the River Wensum to connect Norwich with Great Yarmouth. Yarmouth was and is the county's premier port. Norwich was and is the county's capital. Raw materials went upriver, manufactured goods came down. The so-called "Norwich river" bustled with boats and with business. There were coal sheds and brickyards, maltings and windmills. There were many more boat-builders and ferries and riverside pubs. It is no exaggeration to say that Norfolk's economic prosperity depended upon the Yare.

The walk is well sign-posted.

The wherry Albion *as restored.*

Flag Iris can be found throughout the upper Yare Valley.

The most iconic image of the wherry, taken as the boat effortlessly negotiates the Yare's meanders at Whitlingham.

Now the A47 and the A11 take the strain, leaving the river as a peaceful refuge for pleasure boats and walkers. But look hard and you can still see evidence of the old days. For decades this proud heritage was all but ignored. Then in 2005 the Wherryman's Way was created. On one level the 35 mile route from Norwich to Great Yarmouth simply gave existing footpaths a new name. On another, the information boards and the statues brought the area's history alive to a new generation.

A few months after its launch I was sitting in the White Horse in Chedgrave wondering why no-one had written a book about it. Three pints later my drinking partners Rick and David had convinced me I was the man. Five years on I'm there, but only thanks to the dozens of local people who have willingly shared their knowledge and their enthusiasm with me. The Wherryman's Way is a great route with a great history. Get walking.

Steve Silk
Loddon, 2010

The wherry Albion *in her heyday on Whitlingham Reach*

Walkers find contemplative benches at regular intervals.

The distinctive rig of the wherry Hathor.

9

Chapter 1 Norwich and the Wensum

'All will be well and all will be well and all manner of things will be well.'
Julian of Norwich 1342 to *c.*1416

*"Norwich Thorpe". Norwich City and Norwich Victoria stations did not survive.*

Modern-day Norwich looks down on the river from on high. The heart of the city – the castle, the market and the main shopping streets are all some distance away.

Yet the city started off down here on the banks of the Wensum. And the river remained the city's major link to the outside world for centuries, carrying most of its goods in and out throughout medieval and much of modern times. But less than 20 years after the last grain ship unloaded its cargo at RJ Read's Flour Mill, much of the evidence of those 1000 years is being erased.

For example, throughout that millennium the very idea of fencing off the river, would have seemed ridiculous. But now, just a few hundred yards downstream of Foundry Bridge there is a long sinuous metal barrier between the walker and the Wensum. This, ladies and gentlemen, is the Riverside development. Sailor and docker have been replaced by drinker and clubber. And a succession of drunken people falling to their death, gave the local authorities little choice but to ignore history and play safe.

For many years you crossed the river by either Foundry Bridge at the railway station or Carrow Bridge next to the football ground. But in recent years those road bridges have been joined by two pedestrian ones. The Novi Sad bridge was opened in 2001, the Lady Julian in 2009. The newcomers are helping to change the mood of the river and its surroundings, making it less industrial and more recreational.

Enjoy the bridges, enjoy the people, enjoy the noise. Because for most of our journey it will be big skies, an open river and isolation.

Thorpe Station

It might be Norwich station now. But for most of its 160-odd year life this building was known as Thorpe Station. In the heyday of the railways Norwich had three termini; City; Victoria and Thorpe. Victoria Station lay on the site now occupied by the financial services firm Marsh. City was to the north, behind the inner ring road roundabout near the Halford's cycle shop.

Only Thorpe has survived and decades on, many people still use its original name. The first station building was built in 1844 for the city's first railway – the line connecting Norwich to Great Yarmouth. The structure we see today dates back to 1886.

Opposite: Norwich Castle: the Normans seized the high ground.

The Lady Julian Bridge.

Julian of Norwich – from Norwich Cathedral.

The Novi Sad Friendship Bridge.

The Lady Julian Bridge

The Lady Julian is the latest bridge to cross the Wensum, opening to pedestrians and cyclists during the summer of 2009. Most of the £2.5 million cost came from the developers who have helped transform this part of Norwich over the last decade. What was once a place of work is becoming an area where people rest and play. The Lady Julian is a swing bridge, but it doesn't swing upwards as you might think, but sideways. It was named after the Norwich medieval mystic Julian of Norwich.

Julian of Norwich

Just under 650 years ago a devout 30 year old woman lay on what she thought was her death bed in Norwich. As she lay, she had sixteen visions of the crucified Christ – and was subsequently healed. Later she wrote down her thoughts on what she had seen. Her *Revelations of Divine Love* took twenty years to complete and became the first book written by a woman in the English language. The first, and perhaps one of the most profound. Theologians say that "her perception that there is no wrath in God, but that this is a projection of our own wrath upon him" was centuries ahead of her time.

Once healed, she became an anchorite – a type of hermit living in a cell – at St Julian's Church in Norwich. (Incidentally she is not St Julian, she took her name from the church's patron saint, not the other way round.)

That church was bombed during World War Two, but it was rebuilt afterwards, complete with a chapel on what is thought to be the site of the cell. Now The Lady Julian Bridge spanning the Wensum close to the church, helps her name live on.

Directions to the church: From the Riverside development cross the Lady Julian Bridge. Turn left on to King Street and then immediately right up St Julian's Alley.

Novi Sad Friendship Bridge

When it was opened one newspaper columnist dubbed it the "nowhere bridge", but the Novi Sad at least goes there in style. Technically it is an asymmetric cable stayed swing footbridge, named in honour of Norwich's twin city in northern Serbia. Most of the steel bridge rotates around the central white pier so that larger boats can head upstream when necessary. All of the machinery is hidden inside the pier.

It is elegant, uncompromisingly modern and helped to convince sceptical citizens that something was stirring down on the Riverside in the early stages of the development here. But there is bitter irony in the timing of the bridge's construction. Norwich and

ARCHIVE: *The Ferry Boat Inn*

This much-loved city pub has lain boarded up since 2006. While its future is still uncertain, it has had a proud past. For many decades drinkers enjoyed its low beams, narrow passageways, and the novelty of drinking on many different levels – progressively lower as you got closer to the river.

Its name is no accident. There was a ferry here in the nineteenth century, although at the time the pub was called the Steam Packet. The pub's historian Geoffrey I Kelly tracked down its owners – many of whom were also boatbuilders. Mr Kelly goes on to sum up its character immediately after the Second World War as "a rough, tough, lively house: the haunt in particular of seamen and their time-honoured associates, the local prostitutes".

It had long since lost that reputation before its closure in 2006. But interestingly the area has not. In fact it is arguable that with increased gentrification, soon the only real link with this area's past will be a few last ladies of the night on nearby Rouen Road. While estate agents wring their hands, History quietly has the last laugh.

Top right: The Ferry Boat Inn.

Right: A 19th century photograph of the Ferry Boat Inn when it was known as the Steam Packet. The rowing boat was probably the ferry – complete with ferryman.

Novi Sad's links stretch back forty years. But the bridge was conceived as NATO was bombing what was then called Yugoslavia.

Novi Sad was the hardest hit city – with its three main bridges knocked out by Allied bombers. The Danube, said the locals, was the only river in Europe which flowed over three bridges. But the links between the cities flourished despite the conflict. The bridge in Norwich was opened in 2001 by the Yugoslavian ambassador. And earlier in the same year engineers from Norwich had overseen the restoration of the bomb-wrecked water supply in Novi Sad.

Carrow Bridge

While the Novi Sad looks great and goes nowhere, Carrow Bridge is rather ugly but very useful. As well as a steady stream of cars and lorries, generations of football fans have tramped across it *en route* to Carrow Road. This one is a single-leaf roller bascule bridge – in other words a one-sided drawbridge which uses counter weights to lift itself up.

It was opened by the future Edward VIII on June 27, 1923. The previous bridge had been a little further downstream. Thousands gathered to see the then Prince of Wales open a gate on the new bridge with a golden key handed to him by the City Engineer. Norwich City Football Club have been neighbours since 1935, having flown from The Nest, their previous home in Rosary Road. Sadly the new high-rise flats obscure most of the view of this compact ground from the river. Oh, and "une bascule" is French for a see-saw.

Boom Towers

Carrow Bridge is well worth the one-minute diversion from the Wherryman's Way. Look downstream and you will see stone towers on either side of the river. They are called the Boom Towers, they date back to the 1300s and they formed part of Norwich's city walls. Even today – more than 700 years later – giant chunks of the defences survive along the city's inner ring road. From the bridge, have another look up the hill. Flint and brick remains snake to the commanding heights of Black Tower and beyond.

So why isn't there any evidence of a wall on the Thorpe side of the river? Simply because the river was the wall. The Wensum formed the defensive boundary for the south and the east of the city. We are told that "a chain of Spanish iron" hung between the towers – with a windlass in the western tower. In reality the chain was much more effective as a means of collecting tolls, than it was in holding off waterborne marauders.

Carrow Bridge: New flats look down on an old bridge.

The Boom towers: part of Norwich's medieval defences.

The walls tumble down Carrow Hill.

The Read Mills Housing Development

"Contemporary waterside living within an historic setting," ran the estate agent blurb. Whatever. Norwich was just grateful that anything was being done on the land which lay between the Novi Sad and Carrow bridges. It had previously lain derelict for more than a decade.

The RJ Read flour mill was the most significant landmark here. And the good news is that it was only partially demolished to rise again as Albion Mill. Reads was a family firm which owned mills across Norfolk and Suffolk. The company arrived in 1932, because the site was perfect for sea-going vessels. Brewers, confectioners and carpenters have also been based here over the years. The developers PJ Livesey have chosen their names carefully. There really was a malthouse, a Spooners Wharf and a Half Moon Yard.

From thriving industrial centre to residential quarter; it is just another century of change for the medieval Black Tower to look down upon from Carrow Hill.

Reflections of the past: wharves and mills are replaced by "contemporary waterside living".

People – *Jeremiah James Colman*

Jeremiah James Colman bestrode Victorian Norwich like a Colossus. In a way that would be impossible now, he was simultaneously the city's biggest employer, MP, media magnate and social reformer. And it was his decision in 1854 to move the family business from the village of Stoke Holy Cross to the Carrow Works site, that shapes everything along the river between Carrow Bridge and Trowse. Over the next 50 years this 26 acre site was transformed from a workforce to a community – albeit a community with one leader and no trade unions.

"He was patriarchal in appearance and habits," wrote Colman's historian S H Edgar.

"All the firm's activities centred around his strong personality and nothing took place in the domain of Carrow with which he did not have some concern."

Flour and starch mills were built – which needed granaries and boiler houses. Wharves and wherries followed. And hundreds upon hundreds of workers were sucked in too. The raw materials came by boat. Giant cargoes of mustard seed, cereal and coal were all brought in from Colman's own wharf in Great Yarmouth by wherries.

Amazingly Jeremiah James was not a natural entrepreneur. He could only reconcile making money with the knowledge that he was both employing more people and helping them to live better lives. So in quick succession he built a company school, a dispensary, and a works canteen; all revolutionary in their time. By the end of the century there was also a clothing club, a library, a savings bank, a cookery school, a pension scheme and the Carrow Fire Brigade. You can still see one of the Carrow fire engines in the Bridewell Museum in Norwich. The city came to a standstill for his funeral in 1898. The company continued to innovate and expand after his death and lives on today – on the same site – as a branch of Unilever.

Jeremiah James Colman.

Part of the Colman complex in its heyday.

THE WHERRYMAN'S WAY - DIRECTIONS

The Wherryman's Way starts next to the river at Foundry Bridge – without fanfare. As yet there is no monument for that ceremonial photograph. The river soon turns south, marking the beginning of King Street Reach. It is particularly broad next to the Lady Julian Bridge and that is no accident. This was a turning basin – built to allow larger boats to swing round and head for home.

Left: Parts of the Wensum must now be kept behind bars.

Downstream from the bridge, soak up the view on the far bank. It still looks gloriously messy and industrial. Will this area too be one day colonised by flats? The yards – effectively narrow alleys – run directly down to the river from King Street beyond. They remain full of workshops; although these days it is cars rather than boats which are being repaired.

The "official" Wherryman's Way route says you should cross the river by the Novi Sad bridge. But you get much more of a sense of history by crossing at Lady Julian instead. You emerge onto King Street – arguably Norwich's first ever street. Dragon Hall – a restored medieval merchant's hall and St Etheldreda's church are just two reasons to cross here.

Further down look right up Alan Road to get a glimpse of one of the many towers which formed part of Norwich's walls. A few yards further on the wall crosses King Street itself while Norwich City football club lies on the other side of the river across Carrow Bridge. As we head up hill, everything to our left as far as the Wensum used to belong to Norwich's iconic employer Jeremiah James Colman. Now many of the warehouses have been transformed into flats. Turn left at the traffic lights and head down Bracondale passing the main entrance to Unilever – the current owner of the Colman's brand. Ignore the roundabout and keep heading downhill towards the village of Trowse and Chapter 2.

...As it has been for centuries.

Left: "Gloriously messy" – but for how long?

Below: The medieval timbers of Dragon Hall.

Chapter 2 Trowse

"Holiday time we would all go down to Trowse Common. That was our treat. We'd get up in the morning and the girls and boys would say, 'we're going down to Trowse, are y'coming?'."

Hard Up Street, Growing up in King Street, Norwich, Mary Agnes Davey, 1997

While most of the villages we pass on our way downstream are quiet and perhaps shy, Trowse is exactly the opposite.

Indeed its website declares it to be "the funkiest village in Norfolk, if not the world". It is hard to imagine the people of Claxton or Rockland St Mary, say, making that sort of claim.

Which isn't to knock Trowse, far from it. Norwich might only be a few hundred yards up Bracondale, but the village has brilliantly and fiercely maintained its independence. A school, a shop and two pubs all add to the impression of a community brimming with life.

In earlier days it was a so-called model village. Many of the buildings we see today were built by the philanthropic Colman family – specially for their workers. In earlier times it was also the last call of the drovers leading their livestock up to market in Norwich. They also made use of the now empty Trowse Station.

Finally Trowse is spectacularly green. There might be roads, railways and rivers in every direction, but there is also plenty of open space.

Trowse Mill

Immediately after crossing the first bridge on Bracondale turn right onto a narrow footpath for a five-minute diversion. A mill-like building spanning the river quickly emerges. These flats were built in 2001, but they echo the original buildings which were somehow allowed to be demolished in 1967.

In fact the power of the Yare had been harnessed for centuries. Council historians found one mention as early as 1573 and there was certainly a flour mill in the 18th century. On September 28th 1766 it was besieged by a mob during grain riots in nearby Norwich. The building avoided being ransacked only when the miller offered vast amounts of beer to the men involved.

The whole complex burnt down in 1792. But its owner Daniel Bloome had enough money to rebuild it completely. Photos on the Norfolk mills website show it with two water wheels. We need to return to Bracondale, but the path continues alongside the river. Were you to carry on, you quickly see how road, rail and river all hug this one valley, effectively penning the city of Norwich in to the north.

Trowse Mill: the original building was demolished in the 1960s.

St Andrew's Church

We will see plenty of derelict churches as the Wherryman's Way wends its way to the sea. But 12th century St Andrew's is one which managed to escape that fate – albeit by the skin of its teeth.

"The church is at the present time practically a ruin," wrote church expert Andrew Bryant in the early 20th century.

"On the appointment of the present vicar in 1899, the woodwork everywhere was absolutely rotten so that it crumbled at touch, the floors of the pews had given way and were covered with green moss."

But there was the will to turn it around. Bryant quotes an archdeacon who had said "It is the worst church in the Archdeaconry but it is worthy of the effort and will amply replay the cost of restoration."

St Andrew's Church.

Trowse in the 19th century

Trowse was transformed by one family – the hugely rich, hugely philanthropic Colmans. A poor community became a model village, as Jeremiah James Colman's family invested building by building and street by street.

Their houses survive to this day. The terraces overlooking Trowse Common were for the workers, while larger "villas" were designed for the foremen. A street called The Dell became one of the first areas of sheltered accommodation in the country. As we have seen in Chapter One, Jeremiah James dominated the lives of his workers. He set out to close local pubs, for the good – as he saw it – of his employees.

In a letter of 1892 he wrote: " Since my Firm removed to Carrow they have closed six out of the nine public houses which formerly existed within a quarter mile of the Works ....at Trowse three have been closed out of six which did exist there."

Meanwhile he was busy ploughing his own money into an enlarged school, while the old manor house was being converted into a café and club. But according to Trowse historian Jane Flatt, Trowse was not completely "cleaned up". The drovers bringing their livestock to market would still have given the place a distinctive atmosphere.

Russell Terrace – named after Russell Colman.

"Trowse was the last stop on the drovers' road," she told me.

"And it used to cost a lot of money to stable a horse in Norwich, but not so much here. People would leave their horses here and do their business in the city."

Many people still remember the days when cattle were herded up through the streets into Norwich. Author Mary Agnes Davey grew up in King Street.

"Saturdays used to be a nightmare," she wrote in her book *Hard Up Street*.

"You'd have all the cattle coming down from the market on their way to Trowse Station. ...If they were near the bottom of the market they'd bring them down our way. There'd be thirty, forty, fifty of them all coming along and if you were out on the street you'd run into someone's house it didn't matter whose house, you just got out of the way."

Trowse's pubs

They are down to two pubs in Trowse now, a far cry from its heyday and one fewer than even JJ Colman managed.

The norfolkpubs website can name at least 11 for the nineteenth century. The Hope and Anchor, The Angel, The Britannia, The Pineapple, The Jolly Millers and the Railway Tavern

are all listed as having addresses on Bracondale or Trowse Millgate. For more on The Pineapple see page 23, while The Royal Oak was in the building now used by the May Gurney engineering company, the Railway Tavern was presumably close to the tracks, while the rest lie lost in the mists of Steward & Patteson ale.

In Trowse itself there was The Lime Kiln which might have been on the site of the present day White Horse or possibly on the left-hand side of Kirby Road where Crown House now stands. All of which leaves the two survivors. The White Horse is by far the most convenient for Wherryman's Way walkers. While many pubs change names, this one changed locations. It used to be on the common itself – directly opposite its current spot.

Up the hill on Kirby Road lies the Crown Point Tavern which dates back to the mid 19th century. Its landlady Carol Higgins is quite a rarity – a publican who has stayed at one pub for more than 20 years. We'll explain the American flag on the pub sign when we talk about Crown Point House in Chapter Three, although there is a thorough history lesson in the porch of the pub itself.

Left: The White Horse.

Right: Crown Point Tavern.

Norfolk Ski Club

In all our 35 miles from Norwich to Great Yarmouth there is probably nothing to match this ski slope for sheer incongruity.

Behind us lies a small village. In front of us, the peace and quiet of a country park. But emerging out of the blue on our right is a stonking great ski slope – with a very un-Norfolk gradient.

Norfolk Ski Club was founded in 1972 in a barn alongside the River Wensum in King Street. Founders Ivan Palfrey and Roger and Jennifer Mayhew built a slope out of scaffold poles, wooden boxes and plastic matting. The run was no more than 20 or 30 feet.

Norwich Ski Club.

But it gave "normal" people the chance to have a go at skiing – a rare opportunity in the 1970s. And it was so popular that the club jumped at the chance of moving to this Trowse site a few years later. Crucially it is run by its members – not as a business.

"That's why we've been successful," said Mr Mayhew.

"The sheer enthusiasm of our members means we can continue ploughing the money we make back into the facilities. We haven't got a big enough catchment area to survive commercially."

But as a charity they have gone from strength to strength. They arrived in 1974, ski lifts, a clubhouse and lottery grants soon followed. And when the southern bypass was built in the 1990s, excavated soil was used to further lengthen the slope. Today it is the largest members-run ski club in the country – and there isn't a scaffolding pole in sight.

PEOPLE: *Mike Sparkes*

Mike Sparkes grew up in Trowse in the 1950s. Back then the local children learnt to swim on a stretch of the River Tas known as 'Trowse Beach'. He remembers feeling instantly at home on the water and used to enjoy floating down the river on logs. Later he went on to cox the eights for nearby Whitlingham Amateur Rowing Club and talked of joining the Royal Navy. But it wasn't till he was an engineer in his thirties that this love of the water finally made sense.

Mike Sparkes.

"It was just a chance remark from my mother really. She said her dad used to work on the wherries and suddenly something clicked," he told me.

Within a year this revelation had led Mike to join the Norfolk Wherry Trust – the charity dedicated to preserving and sailing the restored wherry known as the *Albion*. He threw himself into learning everything he could, and almost 25 years later he is both a wherry skipper and trust archivist.

"I've done my family tree and I've discovered that all my family were wherrymen for generations and generations.

"So when you're skipper of the *Albion* there's pride. It's keeping history alive and it's keeping part of our family alive too. When I sail I just do what I feel is right. It comes naturally to me. So yes it just is in the genes."

Mike Sparkes's great-grandfather Stephen Henry Field.

• For more information go to www.wherryalbion.com

THE WHERRYMAN'S WAY - DIRECTIONS

Bracondale continues past the roundabout and into Trowse – or more correctly Trowse Millgate.

Look left. Immediately beneath us is the former Pineapple pub – once beloved of football fans on their way to Carrow Road. Now owned by Norfolk Social Services, it still retains that "corner boozer" look – complete with pineapple motifs high above the doors. If there is something sad about an ex-pub, a deserted railway station is surely even more forlorn. The flint building set further back next to the railway line used to be Trowse Station. It was closed in 1939.

And then it all gets very Victorian. The gabled building with a clockface was opened in 1909 for water board staff who looked after the much taller pumping station to the rear. Peek through a window of this abandoned Edwardian building to see how untouched it remains inside. To the right of these buildings lies their successor. Considerably uglier, the grey metallic shed nevertheless continues with its crucial work of pumping Norwich's sewage to Whitlingham.

Then we cross a young River Yare just before its confluence with the Wensum. This bridge was built in 1863 although some parts are thought to date back to the 15th century. Once we cross the bridge we are in Trowse Newton. The Yare remains the boundary between "City" and "County". Just before St Andrew's Church there is a smaller bridge over a smaller stream. It is a lesser branch of the River Yare – although you could argue it is the last hurrah for its tributary the River Tas.

Trowse now lies straight ahead of us, while we turn left down Whitlingham Lane. The two rivers we have crossed meet under the trees on the other side of the meadows.

Further down Whitlingham Lane look out for Hythe Cottage on the right. You would never know it, but this is another former pub, the Trowse Eye. It was named after the spot where the Yare and Wensum join. To see that confluence, we must keep walking into Whitlingham Country Park ... and Chapter Three.

The Wherryman's Way crosses the young River Yare.

Far left: Trowse station: closed in 1939.

Left: Permanently 8.25: the abandoned water board building.

23

Chapter 3 Whitlingham

"Rejoining the channel, which turns sharply to the right, we see a picturesque cottage, straw-thatched, large-eaved, embowered in trees, clad in creepers, and with a broad dyke in front. This is Whitlingham White House; and from here for about a mile the ground on the right bank is high and wooded, with a ruined church crowning the eminence, and the slopes broken with the old workings of marl-pits."

George Christopher Davies, Norfolk Broads and Rivers, 1884

The new broads at Whitlingham, created by gravel extraction.

Whitlingham Country Park lies within sight and sound of the city centre and yet rarely seems crowded.

It's got the lot. A tranquil stretch of river which has maintained a Victorian charm: centuries of history; mysterious ruins, more than £1.5million of water sports facilities, and a barn converted into a visitor centre. But every inch of wilderness and the sweep of each stretch of water have actually been designed. Whitlingham, you could say, is what happens when town planners get it right.

So geography first, and then history. The Norfolk Broads proper are of course man-made – the product of hundreds of years of peat extraction in the middle ages. Their precise history will be explained when we get to Surlingham Broad. Whitlingham Little Broad and Whitlingham Great Broad are man-made too. But by modern rather than medieval man – and for gravel rather than peat. Millions of tonnes have been extracted since work began in 1990. Much of it has been used on projects close to home – the Castle Mall shopping centre in Norwich for example.

But crucially the gravel extraction was only allowed on condition that the area was looked after properly afterwards. Hence the creation of the Whitlingham Charitable Trust with time (a lease till 2088) and money (a hefty endowment from the landowners) to make something out of nothing.

It is a gentle masterpiece. There will be no waterskiers here. There will be no quadbikes either. The key phrase is "quiet enjoyment": a place to canoe, to birdwatch, to row, sail and walk.

Even advertising its virtues is frowned upon. The Trust's key document includes the wonderful phrase "it is unlikely that it will be desirable or necessary for the Trust to publicise the Park's existence widely." How very Norfolk.

Whitlingham is the first place on this walk where you start to get a feel for how the Yare divides this part of the county. Thorpe St Andrew lies just across the river. But there is no easy way to get there. The ferries are long gone and the only bridge carries high-speed traffic on Norwich's southern bypass. As a result Thorpe and Whitlingham have relatively little to do with each other. That feeling of distinct communities almost ignoring each other, will only grow as we get further away from Norwich.

Top: The outdoor education centre at Whitlingham.

Middle: Outdoor education.

Bottom: Café with a view.

The remains of Trowse Newton Hall.

Trowse Newton Hall

Trowse Newton Hall only exists as ruins now. But over the centuries some interesting lords of the manor have passed through. Priors from a monastery within Norwich Cathedral are the first we know of. They seem to have acquired it a generation or so after the Norman Conquest. It provided them with a rural retreat for centuries. After the dissolution of the monasteries it passed to the deans of the cathedral who later started leasing it out to farmers.

By 1772 the leaseholder was General John Money. He actually lived next door in a new house built in 1784. He named his house Crown Point after a location in the Battle of Valcour Island – a little remembered skirmish during the American War of Independence.

Soldiers don't get more dashing than General Money, a man who seemed to relish danger. After seeing action across Europe and North America, he was back in Norfolk, experimenting with the new-fangled concept of ballooning. The Montgolfier brothers' balloon first took to the skies in 1783. General Money was at it two years later, once having to be rescued from the North Sea after taking off from Norwich. From this point onwards Crown Point became the main "manor house" – with Trowse Newton Hall relegated to working farmhouse.

The banker Sir Robert Harvey then bought Crown Point from an illegitimate son of General Money. The rest of the Money family bitterly contested this decision – a six-page summary of their gripes is still on the shelves of the Millennium Library in Norwich.

Sir Robert was a rich man, and a powerful one too. He was both mayor of Norwich and MP for Thetford. General Money's house was not good enough, so it was demolished to make way for something grander. The whole estate became closed to the public and Trowse Newton Hall was all but demolished - just so that its ruins could look pretty in Sir Robert's garden.

The loss is all the more tragic because by 1870 Sir Robert had shot himself – his great banking prowess uncovered as a sham. In fact he had been secretly speculating on the stock exchange, and forging accounts to cover his losses. The outbreak of the Franco-Prussian war exposed his lies. A history of Norwich banking published in 1900 tells how Sir Robert "lingered three days before he died".

Crown Point – half a mile down the other end of the lime tree avenue – was bought by Jeremiah James Colman, later became Whitlingham Hospital and is now enjoying a new life as apartments. Trowse Newton Hall remains a picturesque ruin – just as Sir Robert had envisaged.

Trowse Eye

The Yare lies to the north of Whitlingham's broads – just beyond the sleek outdoor education centre. From here you can see the confluence of the Yare (coming in from the left) and the Wensum (emerging from Norwich). This is Trowse Eye or Trowse Hythe.

It is almost as if the Yare waits patiently for the Wensum to get through Norwich before the rivers meet. The Yare has flowed quietly through gentle mid Norfolk villages to get to this point: the Wensum – in contrast – has already provided Norwich with its boundaries.

So in many ways this point could be considered a gateway to Norwich. Sadly it looks an ugly mess. The spit of land between the two rivers is occupied by the Carrow Yacht Club - perfect. But a gasometer and two huge electricity pylons ruin the view. If Norwich ever wanted to get serious about attracting waterborne tourists, it needs to take some drastic action here first.

The White House

As Whitlingham Great Broad ends, the Yare snakes down to run close to Whitlingham Lane again. There is an elegant private home here called the White House. This was the site of a popular pub in the nineteenth century, though it is unclear whether that was a previous building or the existing one. One document from 1845 mentions a ferry across to Thorpe here too – pubs and ferries often going together on the Yare.

Left: Trowse Eye – where the Yare and the Wensum meet.

Below: Whitlingham White House in the early 20th century.

The original White House was another victim of Sir Robert Harvey. The best way to continue is to quote William Money – who felt his family had been cheated out of Crown Point by Sir Robert. The document asserting the Moneys' claim, includes a vivid picture of a happy boozer:

"Whitlingham White House, once the idol of pleasure-loving people, is part of the estate, and was in 1861 open to the public, it being a public house at the time conducted by Mrs Digby. Thousands upon thousands have left the smoky old city of Norwich for a row of a few miles down to the grounds to enjoy the fresh air; hold picnics, dance on the grass and indulge in many other amusements; returning home with their lives prolonged at least two or three years. But when Sir R.J.H. Harvey got possession he at once closed it to the public as it remains to the present time. As soon as the necessary questions are settled, however it will be again thrown open."

One hundred and fifty years on we are still waiting. These days thirsty walkers have to wait until the Woods End pub for a drink.

Whitlingham Lime Kilns

A flick through successive Ordnance Survey maps of Whitlingham tells an eloquent story about the changing face of industry here.

Once a lime kiln, now home to bats.

Take the 1907 edition for example. It shows a narrow gauge tramway snaking from the river Yare, round the White House and back into the woods. Local historian Chris Fisher has established that horses would pull wagons filled with chalk from the nearby pits to a riverside wharf. From there wherries would carry their cargo down river. Much went to cement works at Burgh Castle and the Berney Arms.

Today the railway's route still exists – but the quarry face is covered in almost a hundred years of nature. Immediately after the White House turn right through a gate. This path follows the route of the tramway, with both sides growing increasingly steep as you descend. Sit on the bench at the end. Strip away the foliage and imagine.

Take another path further down Whitlingham Lane on the right and you will need the 1886 OS map. It marks the route of an even earlier tramway, again running from the river. The kiln survives.

ARCHIVE: *St Andrew's Church*

Continue along Whitlingham Lane from the kiln, until you see a pair of cottages on the left. Look up into the dense woodland on the opposite side of the road. In the summer you will need to look twice. Amid the greenery lies long-abandoned brick and stone.

These are the remains of St Andrew's Church. The architectural expert Nikolaus Pevsner says the church had not been used since the 17th century. But its round tower collapsed as recently as February 8th, 1940.

"One of my men was going past, " farmer Herbert Matthews told the EDP newspaper, "when he heard a cracking sound – probably the ivy – and then the whole tower going down."

Much of the remains look like they have not moved since. Most are fenced off and there are warning signs. Ignore both – and the thick nettles – and you can discover thick flint walls and fine detail in the windows. Today, it is quite the most improbable spot for a church. And amid the nettle rash and the roar from the bypass, all the more eerie for that.

Top: St Andrew's Church, Whitlingham.

Right: St Andrew's Church – complete with tower.

Chris Fisher worked out that this tram would have run for about three hundred yards. He estimates that together, the tramlines would have been in use for at least eighty years – from the 1840s to the 1920s.

So what exactly does a lime kiln do and why were they so important? Basically it converts chalk (calcium carbonate) into quicklime (calcium oxide) by burning the hewn material. Lime mortar was used by the building trade while quicklime was used by farmers to improve the quality of their soil. In the nineteenth century this was big business.

A chalk pit complete with evidence of the railway in the 1920s.

PEOPLE: *Nobby Clarke and Whitlingham Ferry*

As late as the 1990s there was still a "ferry" marked between Whitlingham and Thorpe on some Norwich maps. In reality it seems as if the rowing boat persisted until the 1960s at the latest.

It was run by Nobby Clarke, remembered now as a "bit of a character" who lived on the Thorpe side of the river in Bungalow Lane.

"He was a diminutive sort of chap, about 5ft tall and he ran a boatyard as well as the ferry," remembers retired river inspector Tony Webster.

Whitlingham ferryman Nobby Clarke.

"He used to do the odd diving job and he would recover bodies from the river too. He got paid more if the bodies were found in the city part of the river than in the county part. So he always said he'd simply move the body to where it suited him!"

Chris Fisher was a teenager at the time. He remembers the staithe being behind Tower Cottage on Whitlingham Lane.

"A lot of people would use it if they wanted a day out from Thorpe. I remember hearing the bell ring on the Whitlingham side and up would pop Nobby to come and collect them."

CIRCULAR WALK 1

DISTANCE: 2 miles

STARTS: Car park at Whitlingham Country Park

Yarmouth Rd

New Cut

River Yare

Outdoor Education Centre

Whitlingham Great Broad

Visitor Centre

Car Park

Whitlingham Country Park

Whitlingham Little Broad

Lime Ave

N
W E
S

DIRECTIONS: From the car park head towards the broad and turn right onto Whitlingham Lane. Soon afterwards take a left turn to get right next to the broad. The Wherryman's Way proper later returns to Whitlingham Lane while we remain at the water. At the end of the broad you can see the River Yare on your right. Our path is now on a narrow isthmus between the two. Look out for the Norwich Frostbites club house on the Thorpe bank, it is one of the few winter sailing clubs in the region. Beyond, a railway bridge crosses what was the original course of the River Yare. The wider "New Cut" next to us was dug out so that wherries did not have to manoeuvre under this bridge and another upstream. The land in between became an island as a result. We return alongside the broad and then turn left at the Outdoor Education Centre. Before you do so however, it's worth continuing for a few yards further to see the confluence of the rivers Yare and Wensum to your right.

Circular Walk 1: The Norwich Frostbites in action.

Take the path between the broads at the education centre and turn left onto Whitlingham Lane to return to the car park.

THE WHERRYMAN'S WAY - DIRECTIONS

Continue along Whitlingham Lane from Trowse and turn left immediately after the canoe club. Then turn right next to the Little Broad. The outdoor education centre at the head of the Great Broad soon appears on the left. The Yare lies beyond these broads and before the high ground of Thorpe St Andrew in the distance. Then look out for the ruins of Trowse Newton Hall on the right, followed by the visitor centre set further back. Our path gets closer to the broad before returning to a narrower Whitlingham Lane which later sidles up to the Yare opposite the White House. A path off to the right here leads to a long-deserted chalk mine. Traffic noise from Norwich's southern bypass gets louder as we continue, passing Tower Cottage on the left and the remains of St Andrew's Church on the right. Go under the bypass and turn left at an unofficial crossroads. The few buildings here are all that remain of the village of Whitlingham. Persevere next to the smelly sewage works on a concrete track and then strike off left onto a sign-posted footpath, across a field and into Chapter 4.

The path down to the old chalk mine.

Chapter 4 Bramerton

"Mount the winding path, to the highest part of the garden and take in at a glance the tortuous course of the Yare and the surrounding country and it will be confessed that the view is a lovely one."

Ernest R Suffling, writing about the Woods End pub in *The Land of the Broads*, 1887

Walkers do not see much of Bramerton village, it is the hamlet of Woods End which nestles next to the river. Drinkers come for the historic Woods End pub while boat owners enjoy the peaceful moorings at Bramerton Common.

In 1828 this part of the river was painted by the Norwich School artist Joseph Stannard. His "Boats on the Yare near Bramerton" captures the tranquillity which survives to this day. More recently it was made famous by a charismatic character from the heyday of the pleasure boat. As the statue in front of the Woods End pub makes clear, Bramerton is Billy Bluelight country. But most importantly for us, Woods End is where the Wherryman's Way returns to the river. Our walk really gets going now.

Above: Winter sunshine at Woods End.

Right: An actor dressed as Billy Bluelight goes racing as the Wherryman's Way is officially opened in 2005.

PEOPLE: *Billy Bluelight*

Billy Bluelight was a one-off – a very Norfolk character who lived on his wits and his charm. He is remembered with a statue here because he used to race the steam pleasure boats along the River Yare.

"What made him so different from the rest was his outstanding personality and his rare standard of behaviour," wrote a local columnist in the Eastern Evening News many years later.

"He had a touching affection and tolerance for mankind and he was always ready to enjoy a joke or to express his opinions at length on any subject under the sun.

When he died in 1949 the Eastern Daily Press received dozens of letters singing his praises. This man's family houseboat was moored every year at Bramerton:

"At half past eleven or so every morning, the tinkle of a harp would intrude upon the cooing of the wood pigeons, heralding the approach of the Yarmouth Belle or the Waterfly with her big freight of Yarmouth trippers bound for Norwich.

"Simultaneously, a strange figure would take up a stance just past the houseboat. Clad in shorts and a singlet, and hung with a prodigious array of medals, his expansive smile seemed to be exactly duplicated at a higher level by the peak of a gaily-striped cricket cap. As the boat drew level there would come a stentorian announcement:

"My name is Billy Bluelight, my age is 45. I hope to get to Carrow Bridge before the boat arrive."

"Off would sprint Billy – medals jingling – along the footpath through the kissing-gates, and across the Common. At the Woods End he would be no more than level, but once out of sight he was able to gain a bit on the short cut across the Whitlingham Sewerage Farm, to reappear neck and neck by the old limekiln at Crown Point. Once more Billy would disappear from view, and while the boat passed very slowly through bends and narrow waters unsuited to her, Billy had to make the detour over Trowse Bridge; but by the time Carrow Bridge was reached (the old bridge by Carrow Works) there would be Billy, ready

to receive the well-earned plaudits of the trippers and the coppers thrown onto the path by the Boom Tower. Year after year the performance was repeated, but Billy's age remained 45! This may have been for the sake of the rhyme, but there was enough of the Peter Pan in him to have justified it on other grounds. Peace to his memory."

Billy Bluelight selling cough mixtures.

William Cullum – to give him his proper name – was also well known on the streets of Norwich. In spring he would be selling daisies or primroses which he described as "Nature's natural flowers"; in the winter it was cough sweets or chestnuts.

His great-nephew Ted Cullum can remember him from the 1930s. Mr Cullum, who was born in 1925, says his family regarded him with both affection and slight embarrassment.

"We seemed to give him a bit of a wide berth. He was one of those people who lived on his wits – he had to.

"I can remember his war cry for the sweets: 'Buy my cough sweets, good for the young, the weak, the old, the wild, the weary.'"

It is a tribute to Norwich's sense of history that he's so well-remembered today – even before the Wherryman's Way statue was erected. Peace to his memory indeed.

ARCHIVE: *The Woods End Pub*

Nothing can beat a riverside pub. But The Woods End is our best surviving example of something slightly different. In Victorian times it was one of several "pleasure gardens" to be found around Norwich. Pubs were for men, but pleasure gardens could be enjoyed by women too. And in the latter half of the nineteenth century, a row or a sail out from Norwich was all the rage.

As it is with houses, so it is with watering holes: location, location, location. A century or so after those Victorians, my first trip on the Broads was in a Hearts Cruiser hired from Thorpe Island. Having negotiated the railway bridge, I remember starting to relax on the long reach down from Postwick Grove. As we adjusted to the Yare's gentle tempo, the Woods End hove into view. Who wouldn't want to stop here?

P H Emerson certainly could not resist in 1890, stopping to beat the locals at skittles.

The Woods End in the 1920s. The pub is set back on the right, a steamer prepares to leave.

"Our game had provoked drinking so the landlord was happy," he wrote in his book On English Lagoons.

"In the bright saloon, with its commonplace tawdry furniture the peasants danced and sang songs, one man singing and accompanying himself by playing a tattoo with his elbow, knuckles, and finger tips."

Perhaps some of the regulars came from Postwick, across the river, certainly there used to be a ferry. Documents from the 1850s call this "The Woods End Ferry Inn" while as late as the 1880s the landlord is listed as "Ferry Owner".

But many more came by pleasure boat from Norwich. The Jenny Lind, The Queen of the Broads and Doris all regularly disgorged passengers here. Today the river remains crucial, bringing about 50 per cent of the pub's business in summer. Location still matters.

Broad + High

On August 18th 1944 a Liberator bomber named Broad + High was returning from its mission in France to its base at Rackheath near Norwich. Badly damaged and short of fuel, it crash-landed in the Kirby Bedon countryside. Four of its crew were killed, three of the remaining five were seriously injured.

Today a plaque to their memory lies at the edge of a copse in a farmer's field just off the Wherryman's Way. Another memorial "To the memory of four gallant American airmen" lies within St Andrew's Church in Kirby Bedon. The men who died were William Sherrill from Tennessee, Darlton W Pontius from Kansas, George Lifschitz from New York and Philip A Snyder from Pennsylvania.

Every fact about their bombing mission to the Aero-Engine works at Woippy near Metz is contained in a detailed book about the 467th Bombardment Group by Perry Watts. Broad + High, he tells us, was named by its crew chief Robert Janton after his home town of Columbus, Ohio. Its two main streets were Broad Street and High Street. The "+" marked their crossroads.

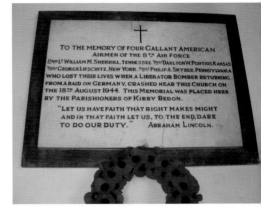

In memory of those who died on Broad + High.

Kirby Bedon's Churches*

Populated now by a congregation of pigeons, the ruins of St Mary's Church in Kirby Bedon still have a certain majesty about them. Unlike the forgotten remains of St Andrew's in Whitlingham (see Chapter 3) these appear anything but neglected. The people of Kirby look after their grounds and the county council has both made the building safe and installed two interpretation boards.

So why does a tiny village have two churches? The theory goes that in medieval times this part of the world was divided up into smaller than usual manorial estates – each one with its own church.

And why did neighbouring St Andrew's "win"? Because St Mary's had come under the control of Langley Abbey in the twelfth century and thus lost out during the Dissolution of the Monasteries in the sixteenth century. St Andrew's became richer, St Mary's fell down.

Today St Andrew's is largely a nineteenth century church. Its own original round tower was pulled down as part of a huge restoration project in the second half of the nineteenth century. Its doors are not often open, but helpful key-holders live nearby. Inside, the church's plaques and notices bear witness to a vast range of history. Look hard enough and you'll find evidence of Cromwell's Commonwealth, the plague, the Great Fire of London, the Indian Mutiny and two world wars.

The ruins of St Mary's church.

* The churches are not directly on the Wherryman's Way. The Way crosses fields from Whitlingham to join the Kirby to Woods End road. You turn left for the pub or detour three-quarters of a mile right to the churches.

PEOPLE: *Mark Wells*

Mark Wells.

The Wherryman's Way is the brainchild of one man – Bramerton resident and former district councillor Mark Wells. His aim was simple: to encourage tourists away from the Bure and the Thurne and help them appreciate the virtues of the Yare.

"Too often the focus is on the Northern Broads," he told me.

"You see the same photos in all the guide books, Horsey, Wroxham etc. That has always driven me mad."

He argued that tourists just needed a nudge in the right direction. Spreading the load would mean the northern rivers were less congested, helping the economy of places like Loddon and Reedham in the process.

"The Yare is a very robust river. It's taken wherries, it's taken coasters, it could easily handle more traffic. The Yare has got space. It's got peace and quiet. It's got some of the best reaches for sailing on the whole Broads. It's just a river that's become neglected over the years."

A change in holiday patterns has also played its part. When holidaymakers spent a fortnight on the water they could cover the entire Broads network – it did not matter where they started.

"Now people tend to come for just three or four days – and then only start from Wroxham. And that can mean there's a vicious circle. Once the boats aren't there to hire, the pubs don't get much trade, etc."

Mr Wells is no longer a district councillor, nor a member of the Broads Authority. But his enthusiasm for the Wherryman's Way remains undimmed. He fizzes with passion about its historical importance.

"The Wherryman's Way gives you a sense of place. It gives you an understanding of why the Yare is so important. Hundreds of years ago Norwich was this country's second city. It had agricultural land around it, production capacity in the city itself and a transport network. Before the railway the Yare was the super-highway of its day and yet almost no-one appreciates that today."

… But his creation means the word is starting to get out.

CIRCULAR WALK 2

DISTANCE: 2 miles

STARTS: Bramerton Common car park

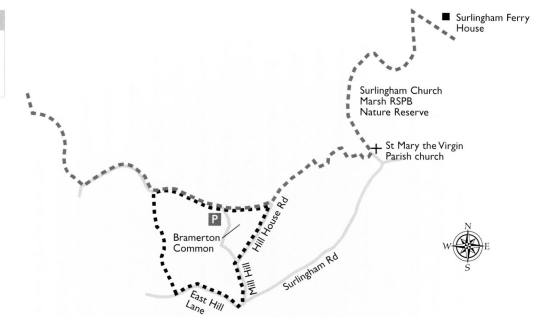

DIRECTIONS: Follow the river along Bramerton Common and then go through a white gate onto a narrow path behind riverside gardens.

At the end of the path turn right up a steep hill passing Hill House on the right. Turn left into Mill Hill down to another t-junction. Turn right here and then immediately right again into East Hill Lane. Pass a bowls club and a village hall before the view opens out across fields. Turn right immediately after Rose Cottage on to a path which heads through a copse and out next to fields. In spring, watch out for a bright yellow crop of daffodils. At the end, turn right onto a road which passes the Woods End pub to return to Bramerton Common.

THE WHERRYMAN'S WAY - DIRECTIONS

It is a relief to leave the sewage works road and step out across country again. Initially the path cuts across farmland before joining a farm track through a small wood.

A field on the left here was where the American bomber Broad + High crash-landed in 1944. The path then descends to the road which connects Kirby Bedon to the river. As you walk towards the Yare you can see alder and willow trees marking out Kirby Marsh, before the road turns to reach Woods End. Watch for traffic, this is still a through road even though it feels like a dead end. As the road bears right up the hill, we continue straight on to Bramerton Common.

Don't miss the Zenith sculpture. What might at first sight look like an abstract work of art is actually highly specific. Lie down on the concrete plinth and look upwards. The copper disc has been drilled full of holes in a painstakingly accurate recreation of the night sky – visible by day.

Our path takes us behind some cottages and then back to the river. You are then faced with a small gate with a confusing message. "Private – Public Footpath" it says. Persevere. You are going to walk around the edge of the garden of Kingfishers Old House. ...And hats off to the owners for allowing us to stay at the river's edge when so many properties force walkers hundreds of yards away from the bank. We'll forgive them the ambiguous notice. I translate it as "Public footpath, but please don't stare at us." Keep going along the riverbank and into Chapter 5.

Top: Circular Walk 2: a field full of daffodils.

Middle: The Wherryman's Way between Whitlingham and Bramerton.

Bottom: Zenith by Barry Mason.

Chapter 5 Surlingham

'For those who are fortunate enough to own or who can borrow a dinghy, the row along the Fleet Dyke is well worth the effort. You will find it a sheer delight in summer to admire the host of marshland flora in full bloom and then to emerge on to the Broad itself with all its bird life.'

Jack Points, 'Surlingham, A South Rivers Village' 1990

Of all the broads, of all the villages, Surlingham is the most untamed. Hidden in its own meander, you never come to this village by accident. The broad too is remote. Wherryman's Way walkers get up close to both Whitlingham and Rockland broads. Of Surlingham Broad, they see precisely nothing.

Which isn't to say that the village has ignored the river and the water – far from it. Wherries unloaded their cargoes at the Coldham Hall pub; there were huge warehouses for coal next to The Ferry House. And within living memory villagers were still harvesting sedge via the parish staithe – which itself still survives. It is just that you have to make the effort to get Broad-side. A canoe is probably the most practical means of transport.

There is a sense of the mystery of history here too. Surlingham has two churches – yet both are some distance from the centre of today's village. Why? No one knows – or is ever likely to know.

The recent past reveals some clues about how acts of God can occasionally wreak huge changes very quickly. Upstream from Coldham Hall is an area known as The Outmeadows. According to Surlingham's historian Jack Points, they used to be grazing marshes. But the great flood of 1912 broke sluices and destroyed windpumps. Ever since, he wrote in 1990, the Outmeadows have been "under water at every tide and the road that led to them has disappeared beneath undergrowth."

Grazing has been re-introduced in some areas of fen more recently however. The RSPB brought highland cattle here in 1998. The charity's aim was to "simulate the way native large herbivores would have maintained open areas in primaeval forests, by grazing year round". Interestingly the experts chose the Highland breed because they could tolerate wet conditions, cold weather and poor quality food.

Crucial clues as to the very origins of the Broads were also found in this area. Scientific detective work carried out in the 1950s helped show that they were man-made. Until then it had been assumed they were natural.

Then there is Wheatfen Broad, another hidden gem. Wheatfen was 'discovered' by the Norfolk naturalist Ted Ellis in 1933. Since then this amazingly diverse fenland habitat has been pored over by experts from across the country.

But – like everything else in Surlingham – it remains peaceful, beautiful and isolated.

Surlingham's churches

Does a small village with two churches including one lonely ruin sound familiar? It happened up the road in Kirby Bedon and it is true of Surlingham too. Although here there is the added mystery of why both churches are stuck out on a limb, some distance from the village centre.

Setting sail from The Ferry House.

St Mary the Virgin.

St Mary the Virgin won the battle for survival. It dates back to the Middle Saxon period, with some historians suggesting it was initially built as a watchtower.

"It is exciting to imagine the invaders," writes the 2006 church guide, "rowing or even sailing round the large bends in the river below the church, and the local people hastening to the confined security of the tower, or trying to make their escape over the high ground towards Norwich."

Sadly, it continues; " But it is interesting speculation without any real evidence to make it more than a romantic idea."

It is certainly a beautiful example of a round tower church, all the more distinctive for its octagonal top. Inside it is spick, span and clearly well-loved. For Yare pilgrims there is even a carefully crafted map of the river, hanging on the north wall. You will see no clearer indication of how the Yare defines, envelops and protects this parish.

Surlingham: in its own meander.

The ruins of St Saviour's Church.

St Saviour's is the church which lost the battle. It lies off the Wherryman's Way, but has to be visited, however sore the feet or late the hour. Turn right through St Mary's lychgate-cum-war memorial and follow the graveyard wall round to the right. Keep going down the path for a few hundred yards and you will find its remains up a few steps on the right hand side.

"The ruins are very picturesque as seen from the river, being mantled with ivy and other creepers" wrote church specialist Andrew Bryant just over a century ago.

"They stand on a gentle slope, and are approached by a typical Norfolk lane … The church never had a tower, but there was one bell which used to hang in a niche on the west wall."

Bryant dates its decline to roughly 1705, but other facts are hard to come by. Even the Pevsner architectural guide calls the church "hard to decipher".

Why were there two churches here? Why did St Mary's survive? We simply don't know. But Surlingham's historian Jack Points made two intelligent guesses. Perhaps there were two separate villages in the Middle Ages, he suggested. And perhaps the Black Death of 1348 – when one in three people died – led to the abandonment of the area around this second church. Alternatively, was the huge flood of 1607 to blame? The Yare Valley suffered badly. Was that the point at which villagers gave up on the low-lying St Saviour's?

Today it's yet another of the Yare Valley's quintessentially peaceful spots, enhanced by the recent graves of Ted Ellis and his wife Phyllis.

Surlingham's secret bunker

There's not much left and it requires a short detour, but history buffs might still be persuaded to see the last remains of Surlingham's secret bunker. During the Second World War, the authorities were very keen to protect the railway marshalling yards at Norwich from the Luftwaffe. So they created a mock yard on the outskirts of Surlingham to lure the Germans further east.

Local people knew something was up on Cross Lane – there was talk of dummy airfields, even dummy Spitfires. But the full truth only emerged as recently as 1992, when the RAF man behind the project revealed all to Eleven Says – Bramerton's local magazine.

John Kent told editor Richard Crosskill that his unit learnt their subterfuge skills at the film studios in Shepperton. The brick building which remains, housed a generator that powered a series of lights across the fields of Surlingham.

Once "Jerry was coming", one set of lights would be switched off. But a set of orange lights, representing those carried by railway engines, were kept on; together with some "mistake lights" for added authenticity. Then with air raids going on above, the RAF's small team would simulate explosions, setting alight mixtures of oil, diesel and water stored in special tanks. And it worked. The logistically important railway yards – and the crucial railway swing bridge over the Yare – survived the war unscathed.

Directions: From St Mary's churchyard, turn left down Church Lane. At its junction with the Bramerton to Surlingham Road, turn right and then first left down Cross Lane. The remains of the building are a five minute walk along this road on the right-hand side. Watch out for an open shaft on top of the building.

The secret bunker.

The Ferry House

The Ferry House.

George Christopher Davies paid close attention to the ferry at Surlingham in his 1884 book *Norfolk Broads and Rivers*.

"It is a large raft worked across from side to side by a windlass and chain, the latter dropping to the bottom when not in use," he wrote.

"It is rather striking to notice how still a horse remains when being ferried across even for the first time, although his eyes and ears show that he is keenly taking in his novel position."

There is a good picture of the ferry on the pub itself to this day. There is no horse, just four passengers along with the ferryman at his windlass, just as Davies describes. Today nothing remains of either ferry or windlass, but the inlaid quay heading next to the flag pole clearly shows where it used to dock.

Surlingham's old "horse ferry".

The ferry was still working when long-time Surlingham resident Millie Reeve moved here in 1936.

"I remember going over there with my bicycle. There was often a sugar beet lorry on there as well," the 87-year-old recalled in November 2007. "The ferry went away during the war – and never came back."

Surlingham author Jack Points interviewed local people for his 1994 book "Chain Ferries Over the Yare". Some remembered horses being led onto the ferry for hunt meetings at Blofield Hall, while others told him that dozens of people came across from pub-free Postwick on summer evenings, lured by either the bar or a small ice cream parlour.

After 1945 what was known as the horse ferry was replaced with a foot ferry. Millie Reeve's son Phil recalls hearing the bell being rung by passengers wanting a lift across in the 1950s.

"Us boys would run down there and we'd get a tanner for rowing someone across. It was a lovely old green boat, a former ship's lifeboat. It would take three of us to do the rowing."

"People used to ride their bike down there to get to Norwich. Cycling through Postwick, you'd be up the city in no time. The sad thing is that there are probably more people commuting to Norwich by bike now than there were back then. If there was still a ferry even more people would do it."

"I'm too young to remember the chain ferry, but I'll tell you that chain is still there on the bottom of the river now."

Memories of how useful the vehicle ferry had been, lingered long in people's memories. As late as 1963 the possibility of it being revived was being mentioned in the *Eastern Daily Press*.

Its roots go back centuries. Historian Geoffrey Kelly found evidence of a ferry here as long ago as 1576. More recently we think that the last landlord to run the foot ferry was Herbert Whitmore. Mr Whitmore – universally known as Simon – was in charge from 1957 for twenty years. He is remembered as a great entertainer who could hold a crowd.

"If there weren't enough people in the pub, he'd go out to the river and get them," recalled Mr Reeve with a chuckle.

"He'd shout to the people on the boats and say 'All the rest of the river is closed, come you in here.'

But that was in the glory days when the Yare was packed with hire boats. These days many publicans find it a lot tougher.

Surlingham's parish staithe

It is the narrowest of dykes and the most humble of moorings, but Surlingham's parish staithe matters simply because it exists at all.

Every village used to have its own staithe at the end of its own dyke, but most have long since fallen foul of weeds, reeds and neglect. It is testament to the days when the people of Surlingham owned strips of the marsh, and harvested them regularly. According to Surlingham resident Phil Reeve, sedge was still being cut as recently as 35 or 40 years ago. Indeed the remains of an old double-ended sedge boat are said to be at the bottom of the dyke to this day.

Sedge differs from reed in that it is flexible. Thatchers use it to form the ridge at the apex of their roofs. The plant is cut in the summer months, being tied into bundles about two feet in circumference. It survives as a commercial crop elsewhere on the Broads, but not at Surlingham. And because it isn't cut, this whole area of marsh is a lot less easy to navigate than it used to be.

Access to Surlingham Broad from this dyke is restricted to Surlingham residents. Other boat users should head upstream from Coldham Hall along the Yare and turn left into Fleet Dyke to Bargate Water. From Bargate, Bird Dyke returns you to the Yare, while another channel heads west into the shallow channels of Surlingham Broad proper. You need a canoe to go much further. You also need a good map and the tide tables. Don't get caught on a falling tide.

Surlingham Broad

If you had been on Surlingham Broad some time in the early 1950s you might have spotted a woman in a boat, armed with very long, very narrow pipes.

Her name was Doctor Joyce Lambert and her painstaking work was about to change our understanding of the history of the Broads. The pipes were in fact a device for collecting soil samples beneath the water. She and her team sank thousands of them at locations across the Broads.

The process is lovingly described by fellow scientist Brian Moss in his 2001 book "The Broads". You take a four metre pipe of about eight to ten centimetres in diameter and cut it in half longitudinally. Then you tape it back up again with waterproof tape.

"It helps if the bottom end is sharpened for easy penetration, for you stand in a very well-anchored boat, eventually on the thwarts of it, and push the tube as far into the deposits as you can," wrote Professor Moss.

Once you reach five centimetres of peat, you can pull it up again. The peat acts as a temporary plug until you can get a proper rubber bung in. Then there is the small matter of getting rid of the water on top which the professor says he has survived "with dry humour if sodden clothes".

Peace reigns at the Parish Staithe.

Dr Joyce Lambert taking samples with a hand-boring tool in 1952. Her research revolutionised our view of how the broads were formed.

One split down the waterproof tape later and "displayed before you will be several centuries of ecological history."

"Sometimes it will appear as several shades of amorphous dark brown ...but more usually in the Broads you will be presented with a sequence of different-coloured layers like a block of Neapolitan ice cream."

Dr Lambert's conclusions from this work were startling. The sides of the broads were vertical faces of undisturbed clay or peat, while the bottoms were horizontal. Lambert realised that these "natural" lakes were actually former peat diggings. Centuries of overgrown vegetation had hidden their peculiar shape.

After that, it was a case of working with historians and archaeologists to establish whether this could actually be true. Evidence soon emerged that turf cutting was indeed carried out on a huge scale in the middle ages. The resulting book was what Professor Moss calls "a spectacular coup of interdisciplinary scholarship" with five experts providing evidence from their different fields.

"The Making of the Broads" was truly revelatory when it was published in 1960. Dr J M Lambert – who died in 2005 – deserves a place in the pantheon of Broads' greats.

ARCHIVE: *Coldham Hall Tavern*

If wherries were the HGVs of their day, then the pubs of the Yare were the transport cafes. They were friendly, familiar places where those with business on the river met, ate and drank.

And of course most pubs provided transport for local people too – in the form of a ferry. But the Coldham Hall Tavern takes this intimate connection with the Yare one step further. For it was originally a pub-cum-ferry-cum-boatbuilder's yard – a true Broads holy trinity.

Indeed in the 1920s, when boatbuilder and shipwright Billy Breach decided to move on from Oulton Broad, he was attracted to Surlingham by the boatyard, not the pub. He became master of both. And thus began a family association with the pub which lasted fifty years – while the connection with the boatyard continues to this day.

His grand-daughter Mary Upton still runs W J Breach & Sons from the boatsheds immediately upriver from the pub.

The ferryman at Coldham Hall.

"My grandfather and my father came here in 1921," the eighty-three year old recalled when I spoke to her in December 2007.

"They repaired the wherries, they built river boats – motor cruisers that sort of thing – and they also built ferries. My father Harry Last took over the pub in 1953 and carried on till 1973. That was when the ferry stopped running too."

Unlike the Ferry House, this was only ever a passenger ferry – a large rowing boat.

"People used to use it to catch the train at Brundall or go to the doctors. Once I was aged about ten or so, I used it every day to get to school in Norwich by train."

A postcard shows youngsters fishing from the Brundall side of the Coldham Hall jetty. The swans were drawn on by the person who sent the card.

"There was a bell on either side of the river for passengers to ring and I remember it cost one old penny to get across. Anyone who was around would do the rowing – which they always did standing up. Sometimes it was a member of the family, sometimes it was one of the men who worked at the boatyard."

In earlier days it was very busy – almost inconceivably busy from our perspective. Surlingham author Jack Points spoke to a man called Reginald Clough who had worked the ferry in about 1912. Each passenger was charged a penny and the boat could carry 14 people.

A Coldham Hall wherryman – his pint is always full.

"From midday Saturday till about 10pm on the Sunday he would take about 35 shillings in fares, for which he was paid 10 shillings," he wrote.

"This means he would have carried over four hundred people across the river."

Coldham Hall wasn't just a pub. There were tea rooms too. The buildings were demolished in the 1970s. But they are a reminder of just how popular this stretch of river used to be.

"My mother and grandmother used to do the teas," recalled Mrs Upton.

"There used to be a boat called Doris which came up from Norwich, full of people on board. Sometimes people would stay the night too."

- Just finally Coldham Hall has the most Norfolk of addresses. It is "Coldham Hall Tavern, Coldham Hall Carnser, Surlingham." A carnser is the local dialect word for a raised road or causeway. Look carefully and you will see that either side of the road is marsh. After heavy rain, the carnser only just does its job.

The Yare Navigation Race

Sail isn't yet a rarity on the River Yare. The infectious lure of windpower still attracts hundreds of people.

Sunday mornings are particularly popular, with the sailing clubs out in force. Wind-blown triangles of canvas criss-cross the river from the Frostbites of Thorpe St Andrew to the Buckenham Sailing Club at the Beauchamp Arms.

And yet as you walk alongside a stretch of river at any other time of the week, you are much more likely to see a boat powered by an engine than by the wind. But all that changes on one Saturday every September with the Yare Navigation Race. Typically between 60 and 70 river cruiser class boats compete, sailing from Coldham Hall Sailing Club down to Breydon Water and back again. The distance varies according to where the mark is placed on Breydon, but it is usually at least thirty miles. There is a precise definition of a "river cruiser". Basically it means a boat with bunks, a galley and a loo – in other words a boat capable of being lived on.

"A good river cruiser with a competent crew will do it in between four and six hours, depending on the conditions," explained YNR organiser Geoff Pinder.

"People say it is the most challenging race on the river, but others call it 'high-speed ditch crawling'. People do break their masts and others run aground. But it's the one race that people will come from miles around to take part in. The important thing is getting all of those boats on the river on one day."

• For photos of the Yare Navigation Race see the Reedham chapter.

Right: Coldham Hall sailing club.

PEOPLE: *Ted Ellis and Wheatfen*

"As important in its way as Mount Everest," is a bold way to describe anything, let alone a remote swamp in the back of Norfolk's beyond.

Yet that is naturalist David Bellamy's claim for Wheatfen. It is all the more remarkable since its high profile is entirely down to the single-minded devotion of one man – Ted Ellis.

Edward Augustine Ellis 'discovered' Wheatfen in the 1930s. A born naturalist, he became Keeper of Natural History at the Castle Museum in Norwich in 1928. One day in 1933 he fell into conversation with a museum visitor. Captain Maurice Cockle had come from a remote fen near Surlingham with a collection of shells.

"It was a turning point in Ted's life," explains Eugene Stone in his biography "Ted Ellis the People's Naturalist".

"For, unbeknown to the captain, his land – from a scientific point of view – proved to be 150 acres of the richest, most diverse fenland habitat in East Anglia."

Many years later – after Captain Cockle had died – the Ellis family moved into Wheatfen's rundown marshmen's cottages, and never looked back. The study of Wheatfen became Ted Ellis's life's work, proving as Stone writes "that the more closely you look at something small – even the piece of ground between your feet – the more there is to see."

As a result Wheatfen became the best-recorded fen in Britain.

The man himself died in 1986, but his work goes on to this day thanks to the Ted Ellis Trust. Wheatfen remains a nature reserve, one of the last tidal marshes of the Yare Valley.

continued...

Ted Ellis – the naturalist.

Above and overleaf: Wheatfen: Ted Ellis's paradise on earth.

The Trust says it wants to preserve the rich and fragile ecology while keeping it all accessible to the public. Non-naturalists should not be put off. Yes, there is a complex mix of open fen, reed beds, sallow carr and small broads for the knowledgeable to enjoy. For the rest of us, it is just an incredibly unspoilt place of beauty and peace.

As Ted Ellis said of the Broads in general, Wheatfen remains "a breathing space for the cure of souls".

CIRCULAR WALK 3

DISTANCE: 1½ miles

STARTS: Small car park opposite Surlingham Church

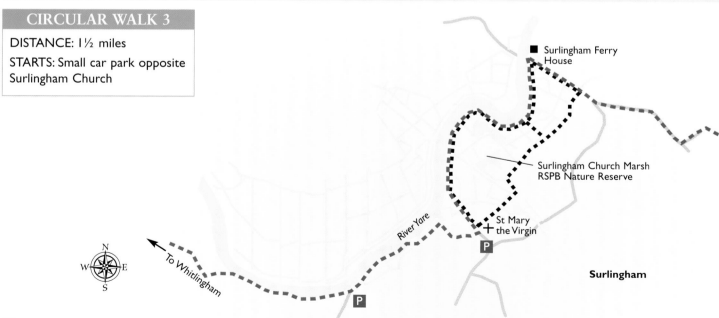

Surlingham Ferry House

Surlingham Church Marsh RSPB Nature Reserve

St Mary the Virgin

River Yare

To Whitlingham

N
W E
S

Surlingham

DIRECTIONS: Turn right out of the church and take the footpath to the left of a cottage to head downhill to the river. Follow the river, passing a bird hide until you reach the Surlingham Ferry House Inn. Turn right up the road away from the pub and then turn right again onto a footpath. Cross a number of stiles, eventually passing a gun club on your left. Later look out for the ruins of St Saviour's Church up some steps, again to the left. This track returns to St Mary's church. Honey is often for sale en route.

THE WHERRYMAN'S WAY - DIRECTIONS

As you look downstream from Bramerton you might get the impression that nothing could drag the Wherryman's Way away from the river along this stretch. Sadly the illusion doesn't last long. A few houses with stubbornly big gardens get in the way.

Views disappear amid thick undergrowth and ninety-degree turns between gardens, until it is quite a surprise to emerge directly opposite St Mary the Virgin's church on the western fringes of Surlingham. Turn left and head downhill until we're back where we belong. This – as the helpful noticeboard in the graveyard explains – is Church Marsh Nature Reserve.

The RSPB reserve is only small, but it includes reedbeds, fens and pools as well as a reed screen and a hide for birdwatchers. There are no diversions, no restricted views and the only funny turn comes from the Yare itself, as it twists into and out of a horseshoe bend. Look right to see the remains of St Saviour's Church in the distance. After drinks at the Ferry House Inn, turn right along the metalled road away from the river. Notice how it is pretty much a causeway with swampy carr on either side. Watch out for the sign to the parish staithe on the left. Apart from that short detour to the staithe, there are no footpaths along either the river or the broad here, so the Wherryman's Way is forced onto a road called The Common. Then take a left down a sign-posted footpath towards the river, emerging at Coldham Hall Tavern. From there walk through a car park to Coldham Hall Sailing Club enjoying the views across to Brundall. From the club, the path turns away from the Yare again, eventually rejoining The Common.

The main road soon turns right, but we continue in a straight line turning onto a more minor road. This is The Covey, named after a chunk of Surlingham Wood which we will come to shortly. Brickyard Farm, further down on the left, was the site of one of two brickyards in Surlingham. The finished products were of course shipped by wherries from a special staithe.

Next up lies Ted Ellis's home – Wheatfen. The road runs out at this point, but the path continues in the same direction skirting The Covey. Turn right at the end of the field and then left through a hedge to Broad Hall Farm, the village of Rockland and Chapter 6.

Circular Walk 3: honey for sale.

Back on the river bank.

Chapter 6 Rockland St Mary

"Punting homeward from Rockland Staithe late this evening I drew into the shade of a willow tree and enjoyed for a few moments the utter peace of Broadland. The waters seemed to have a frozen stillness and with the discs and upturned edges of lily leaves, the spiky blackness of the reeds at dusk, the silhouettes of herons and great noctule bats against the sky and the pure silver of the great expanse of Broad, I was reminded of the prettiest artistry of Japan..."

Ted Ellis, *Eastern Daily Press* article, May 28th, 1948

Rockland Staithe.

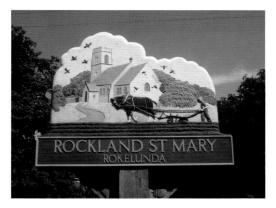

Left: These "timbers" at Rockland Staithe represent the sunken wherries in Rockland Broad.

Rockland truly is a "great expanse of Broad", the biggest we'll encounter until Breydon Water right at the end of the Yare's voyage to the sea.

And even here in its middle reaches the Yare is changing. The valley opens up past Surlingham. There are fewer trees and more marshland; fewer kingfishers, more warblers and harriers. We start to see the classic East Anglian big skies – what writer James Wentworth Day called "an ancient and unspoilt valley of great skyscapes and green and brown landscapes where clouds sail like galleons".

On the Broad itself lie some more recent galleons. The sad remains of a dozen sunken wherries are known as The Slaughters and are sometimes eerily visible at low tide. Everything is getting a little bit more open to the elements.

Even Rockland's most famous character is wilder. James "Old Scientific" Fuller was the last of the wildfowlers to live on a boat and survive by the rod and the gun. We are told he used to drink prodigiously at The New Inn by Rockland Staithe – a pub which survives and prospers with a more refined clientele. And the Wherryman's Way gets back to the water at the pub and stays there for as far as the eye can see.

The New Inn

Another "location" pub, the New Inn provides the most welcoming of views to anyone arriving by boat at Rockland Staithe. It appears to date back to at least the 1850s and originally included a skittle alley and stables.

Rockland used to have three pubs – The Star on Star Lane and another called The Crown. Only The New Inn remains, undoubtedly because of its waterside location. Successive generations of wherrymen have been followed by successive generations of tourists.

The New Inn.

PEOPLE: *Old Scientific*

James Fuller has only been dead for eighty years and yet he has already become something of a legend. Better known as "Old Scientific" he was pretty much the last of the wildfowlers to make a living – indeed make a life – from the broad itself.

He cut reeds, he fished and he shot. And when other people tried to do the same, this self-styled "King of Rockland Broad" was not above shooting at them too. James Wentworth Day was one of several writers who started to lionise him in the years after his death in 1928.

Old Scientific.

"A man of sharp tongue, quick talk, quick eye and a majestic thirst," he wrote in a 1949 magazine article.

"He could shoot like a cock-angel, skate like a dream and shoot a bird on the wing while skating at full speed. He caught fish when other men went home empty and mourning. He speared eels, snared pike, and spied fowl with the eye of a falcon, stalked them with the cunning of a fox. He called no man master."

In another article he talks of a thirst for beer quenched at the New Inn.

"And then rattling his hob-nailed leather water boots on the stone floor, he would dance a wild jig which struck sparks from the flags and end up by challenging any man there to fight him for a quart."

Yet firm facts about Fuller are hard to come by. Despite his graphic language Wentworth Day never met him in the flesh – although he certainly talked to others who had.

James Fuller died on January 6th 1928 at the age of 79 – away from Rockland in the village of Swainsthorpe. A very short obituary in the East Anglian Daily Times later that month said "although he had not slept in a bed for nearly sixty years, he died in one." On his death certificate his occupation is given as "waterman". The cause of death was pneumonia, with "chronic alcoholism" as a secondary cause.

The only writer definitely to have met him was W A Dutt who was writing at the start of the 20th century. Dutt says that Fuller lived in a cottage within a stone's throw of the Broad. But he spent much of his time afloat in a "slate-coloured punt" hunting everything from bitterns and spoonbills, goosanders and duck.

"So long had been his acquaintance with the Broad, that almost every reed and gladden bed, sallow carr, creek and dyke, reminded him of some gunning experience," he wrote.

Everyone's favourite Scientific story sees him challenged to shoot a gull while skating at full speed on an icy Broad.

"He waited till the gull wheeled above him. He then skated after it, soon abandoning his usual stroke for that rapid run on skates which the Broadsman resorts to when he wishes to attain a considerable speed. Then his gun went quickly to his shoulder, and a moment or two later the gull dropped almost at his feet."

He was probably a cantankerous old so-and-so with plenty of enemies. But history has decided to smile upon him.

But how many locals or tourists realise it also helped provide a composer with the inspiration for one of his best-loved works?

Ernest John Moeran was born in 1894 and grew up in Bacton on the Norfolk coast. His music is not well known, but he has a hardcore of dedicated fans.

A website in his honour describes him as "the greatest unsung genius of English composition. His music, often lost in the noise and hubbub of the 20th Century, is that of a uniquely beautiful lyricism, capturing feelings and rural landscapes in a way no other composer ever has."

Moeran's father was Irish and he enjoyed exploring those roots. But his Fantasy Quartet for Oboe and Strings saw him fall back in love with the Norfolk he had known as a child.

"I board and lodge in this little pub overlooking Rockland Broad," he wrote to a friend.

"In the evening I go out rowing on these 'Lonely Waters'... this reedy neighbourhood seems to suggest oboe music".

The *Times* critic described it as 'Sunshine over rural England' when it was first performed in 1946. The Wherryman's Way has a soundtrack at last ...

Rockland Broad from the Yare: look hard and you can find most of P H Emerson's lost dykes.

Rockland Broad

Rockland Broad is a pleasantly complicated bit of water with channels and dykes heading off in all directions. It is not that deep so boat owners beware on a falling tide. From the north it is connected to the Yare by Fleet Dyke, a long straight finger which dips into the Broad at its tip. From the south there is Short Dyke which Wherryman's Way walkers stroll alongside to rejoin the Yare.

Historically there were at least five more channels. P H Emerson, writing in the 1880s says "the Broad debouches into the river by seven mouths, locally called Fleet Dyke, Rockland Dyke, Black Dyke, Big Sallow Bush Dyke, Little Sallow Bush Dyke, Jerrymarsh Dyke and Short Dyke".

View from a canoe: one of the islands formed by a sunken wherry.

Left: View from a canoe: part of a wherry emerges at low tide.

Right: Early morning in spring on Rockland Broad.

By 1902 the writer Nicholas Everitt was talking of "the three entrances to Rockland Broad". Today there are definitely only two.

The area between them is known to RSPB staff as "The Island". The charity is in the process of removing acres of scrub from this area. The idea is that once the willow and the sallow are removed, other plants and insects will flourish because they will not be "shaded out". Ditches that have not been touched for one hundred years will be cleared. It should be good news for – among others – bitterns and swallowtail butterflies. Elsewhere a channel heads north west into Wheatfen Broad while another to the south west connects the Broad to Rockland Staithe and the New Inn.

But the most poignant part of Rockland Broad is The Slaughters – the graphic name given to the decaying remains of 13 wherries sunk in one long line to protect the main channel. Star of Hope, Gleaner, Unexpected, Diligent, Chieftain, Providence, Cambra, Madge, Tiger, Empress, Leverett and Myth are the ones we know about. The hulk of one more craft lies unidentified at the southern end.

This graveyard for wherries is only visible at low tide – and from the water. From my canoe I have watched small summits of timber slowly emerge from the depths – and been suddenly grounded by others still hidden. And on my desk as I write, I have a 27 inch long bolt liberated from one of those carcasses – Chieftain perhaps or maybe Providence. They built those wherries well. It will be a few years yet before they disappear for good.

The Rockland Broad case

In May 1908 two members of the Norwich Angling Club walked into the petty sessions court in Swainsthorpe. Their "crime" was to fish at Rockland Broad and the man accusing them was the lord of the manor there, Sir Charles Henry Stuart Rich.

Rockland Broad was his, the men had acted unlawfully, and it was such a grave case that action had to be taken under the Larceny Act, he argued.

But, as in all the best court stories, the toff gets turned over by a firm but fair magistrate. And the Rockland Broad case ended up being an important victory for the common man. The anglers' defence team successfully argued that the broad was tidal. And the chairman of the bench Lord Lindley concluded that under Common Law the anglers did indeed have public rights to both navigation and fishing. Rockland Broad was free to all and Sir Charles never did prove that he owned it.

Lord Lindley's decision had far-reaching effects. Rockland was to become the only broad not in private hands. The only broad therefore where people could shoot as well as fish. And over the years people have done just that. Indeed it got out of hand. As recently as the early 1980s, the first day of the wildfowl season would see dozens of boats heading out onto the Broad. The situation was only resolved by the creation of the Rockland Wildfowlers Association.

Rockland Wildfowlers Association

There are modern day equivalents of Old Scientific and they still stalk their prey on Rockland Broad. They are not universally popular in the 21st century, but there is a fierce determination to continue with a long tradition.

"This is not game shooting, that's the first thing to remember," says RWA secretary Aidan Ward.

"With game shooting, the birds have been reared to be shot. But with wildfowling you're talking 99.9 per cent wild birds."

"The last eight times I've got up at 4.30 am and gone shooting I've come back with a total of two ducks. This is not wholesale slaughter."

So what is it all about? Wildfowlers will tell you it's about pitting their wits against ducks and geese. They also talk about seeing nature at its best; witnessing a wide variety of wildlife and wanting to eat meat which has not been factory-farmed.

As the RWA website says: "Most wildfowlers shoot for the pot and not to see if they can out-shoot their neighbour – in any event what's the point of shooting more birds that you can comfortably carry the half mile or more back to the car across several marshes?"

The Rockland Wildfowlers Association was set up in 1985 amid fears that shooting was about to be lost altogether. Until that point it had been a free for all.

James Wentworth Day, writing in 1950, summarised it with his usual hyperbole:

"The shooting on Rockland is free, and thereby it is a highly dangerous place. Go there at early dawn on the opening day of the duck-shooting and it is ten to one that you will receive the better part of an ounce of shot, for they distribute their leaden largesse with a fine, open-handed, undiscriminating generosity....Not that that worries the Rockland villagers. They, one hears, are born armour-plated."

By the 1980s it was clear something had to be done. And in the end about 30 wildfowlers started talking to the local councils about regulation. The result is today's – very stable – compromise. The RWA limits itself to two days a week shooting. Its members look after the environment and keep records of everything that gets shot. It is all very scientific, if not Scientific.

The Mid-Yare Nature Reserve

This is a nature reserve with a scale that is difficult to comprehend by humans, but makes perfect sense for birds. On our side of the Yare it runs almost continuously from Church Farm at Surlingham down as far as Short Dyke at Rockland. On the other side of the river it is even more extensive, covering a vast area from Strumpshaw through Buckenham to Cantley.

Thus a huge chunk of the middle reaches of the Yare is protected. Every habitat is represented here. Broads, dykes, fen, grazing meadow and alder-willow woodland are all looked after from the RSPB's base at Strumpshaw.

"The great thing is that we have plenty of documentation about what used to be here," explained site manager Tim Strudwick.

"In many ways this was the most accessible part of the Broads in the Victorian days. People would come up from London and use the stations at Brundall and Buckenham to visit places like Surlingham, Strumpshaw and Rockland."

"And because we've got that documentation we know what we've lost. And somehow that makes it easier to at least try and get some of it back. We also had Ted Ellis up the road as well of course. So some of this area has been in conservation for a long time."

St Mary's Church, Rockland.

Strumpshaw attracts 15,000 visitors a year while another 5000 pass through Church Farm at Surlingham. There are no numbers for Rockland, but the trend here is definitely up – spurred on at least in part by the advent of the Wherryman's Way.

Some in Surlingham complain that there is no longer a warden on their side of the river. The RSPB counters that it is spending big money there. Certainly much has been done on both sides since the Mid-Yare was created in 1997. And from a bird's eye view it certainly seems to make sense.

Rockland's churches

Once again we have two churches in one village, indeed two churches in one graveyard. St Mary's Church is today's parish church, while the flinty remains of what used to be St Margaret's lie right alongside.

St Margaret's dates back to the 14th century when the parish was called Rockland Minor – with St Mary's being Rockland Major. It is thought that St Margaret's has been a ruin for at least 300 years.

Both lie just off the Wherryman's Way circular walk, but a good mile from the main walk.

CIRCULAR WALK 4

DISTANCE: 7 miles

STARTS: Rockland Staithe car park

Surlingham Ferry House

Surlingham Church Marsh RSPB Nature Reserve

River Yare

St Mary the Virgin

Surlingham

Strumpshaw RSPB Nature Reserve

River Yare

Ted Ellis Trust at Wheatfen Nature Reserve

Rockland Broad

Rockland St Mary

N
W E
S

Circular Walk 4: Abandoned machinery near Holloway Road.

DIRECTIONS

From the staithe walk up the hill to The Street. Continue past the post office before turning right onto a footpath between houses, before an electricity sub-station. This path emerges onto fields. Turn right and then left along a line of conifers. Continue to follow the field-edge path towards Surlingham, eventually emerging onto Holloway Road.

Turn left passing a disused barn, and then right onto Cross Lane. Look out for Chapter 5's secret bunker in a field on the left. Go straight over at the junction onto a footpath which soon turns right and emerges next to Surlingham church. Turn left and follow the graveyard round to the right, passing the remains of St Saviour's church. Follow the path across a board walk and several stiles to reach Ferry Road.

From here we are on the main Wherryman's Way. Turn right and take the left fork onto the Common and left again to Coldham Hall. Pass the sailing club and then take a path away from the river back to The Common. Turn left and continue onto

The Covey when the main road turns right. This track becomes a path passing the Wheatfen Nature Reserve. Follow the field, eventually turning right along the hedge and then left towards Broad Hall Farm and onto Green Lane. Turn left onto New Inn Hill to return to the car park.

THE WHERRYMAN'S WAY - DIRECTIONS

This is the one stretch of the walk where the Wherryman's Way is more direct than either river or road. The footpath from Broad Hall Farm described in Chapter 5 quickly becomes Green Lane. You then pass a picturesque children's playground before emerging on to the main road. Head left down the hill to the New Inn and Rockland Staithe. After drinks at the pub, take the track to the right of the dyke and head towards Rockland Broad. We are now on an easy access path which skirts the southern edge of the Broad. The odd "RWA" sign will be the only indication that this is the home of the Rockland Wildfowlers Association.

The spot close to today's bird hide is known as Mill Corner. Watch out for the remains of a cast iron windpump mechanism on the right. It belonged to a mill which helped drain the marshes here a century ago.

The path soon turns an abrupt right as we leave the broad along Short Dyke – one of two navigable dykes between the broad and the river. We are soon back on the Yare. Just upstream on the north bank lies Strumpshaw Mill engine house - probably dating back to the 1830s. Directly opposite in the distance is Buckenham Halt, one of the smallest railway stations in Great Britain.

The footpath continues along the river with the modern Claxton Pumping Station providing a convenient punctuation point into the next parish – and the next chapter.

Rockland Short Dyke.

Left: The original mill next to Rockland Broad.

Below: All that remains of Rockland mill.

Chapter 7 Claxton and Carleton

"Whenever I reach for the boots and binoculars and head out of the door I could go in any direction from the house to find wildlife. Yet something hard-wired in my brain means that the internal compass always trends to the River Yare, or some offspring body of water that eventually makes its sluggish meandering course back into the parent further downstream."

Claxton resident Mark Cocker in "Crow Country", 2007

The Beauchamp Arms with the masts of Buckenham Sailing Club.

Claxton's big claim to fame is its castle, but forget any notions of a grand building commanding the high ground. Instead the remaining walls lie pretty much at marsh level, easily overlooked amid the grounds of the private manor house and farm which have grown up around it. Could it be the lowest castle in the country?

Both castle and village lie some distance from the Yare and since the Wherryman's Way sticks to the river here, walkers will have to complete the circular walk to see either the village or its oldest building.

Carleton St Peter is Claxton's diminutive neighbour. Its population might only be thirty-something, but it still manages to pack a pub, the site of an ancient ferry, a sailing club and an extinct broad into its compact borders. Both village churches lie semi-detached from their populations; a mysterious but common theme in the Yare Valley – and indeed Norfolk as a whole.

ARCHIVE: *Claxton's railway*

This stretch of river looks so desolate and so lonely it is hard to imagine it once being a hive of activity for man and machine.

Yet as recently as 1936 a one-mile stretch of narrow gauge railway crossed the marshes here between Manor Farm and the Yare. Farmer John Pyke built it to carry his sugar beet crop down to the river. The railway's locomotive was a Model T Ford. Or rather a Model T Ford welded on top of a cannibalised wagon …with the help of some sprockets and chains from a sail-binding machine and the expertise of a nearby foundry.

Farmer Pyke's railway circa 1928: For Claxton's annual fete the train was used to take villagers down to the river. Billy Mason is in the driving seat.

It is just the kind of fascinating detail which might have been forgotten forever had it not been for local historian Chris Fisher. He stumbled across the story in 1984. Painstaking detective work led him to a retired farm steward who – he had been led to believe – might just remember the railway.

"Indeed he did," wrote Mr Fisher in a later article, "and he suggested that I go and interview the driver!"

Billy Mason still lived in Claxton. He had worked for the farmer between 1923 and 1941 as an agricultural engineer.

continued…

He could recall the two-feet track being laid in pre-fabricated sections in about 1926, curving right once it reached the river. He could also remember the long pine tree bridges which allowed the railway to cross the drainage dykes and a ten-foot turntable at either end of the line. The Model T had kept its gearbox and its petrol tank under the seat, while a canopy was added to give it more of a "loco" feel. The livery, notes Mr Fisher, was "sort of black and rusty".

About two years later the railway was extended for a further half mile beyond the farm – effectively to the fields themselves. But by 1936 the line was quickly becoming obsolete as lorries came into general use. In time of course the rise of the lorry would also spell the end of the Yare as a commercial artery.

Billy Mason died soon after Chris Fisher had spoken to him. Between them they had ensured that another colourful chunk of Yare history would not be forgotten.

The most substantial remaining wall of Claxton Castle.

Claxton Castle

One writer called it the castle 'that history has forgot'. Another complained of how difficult it was to find along "devious narrow lanes" far from the beaten track. But of course the point about Claxton Castle is that it was built to be approached by water rather than by road. Today it is set back a little from the river because the Yare in medieval times used to run much wider and wilder. The building is not open to the public. It forms part of the grounds of Claxton Manor. But walkers on the main road through Claxton get a clear enough view of some still substantial walls.

For more than a century everyone has dated it to the early 14th century because it was then that the de Kerdiston family were given a licence to crenellate it. But a more recent study has come up with a much earlier date. Dr Thomas C Welsh surveyed the castle in 1995. He found a mention in a document of 1198 which "implied" a castle. And he also argued that the evidence on the ground suggests there could have been something here as early as Saxon times.

You need very good eyes to see the walls from the Wherryman's Way walk along the river. The circular walk gets much closer.

St Andrew's Church, Claxton.

St Andrew's Church

The countryside around Claxton might be sparsely populated, but it does include a wonderful warren of tiny roads and a surprising number of churches.

Amazingly, there are four within a mile of St Andrew's: St Peter's at Carleton; St John the Baptist at Hellington; St Mary's at Ashby and St Mary's at Rockland. (In fact there used to be a fifth, yet another St Mary's in the "lost" village of Holverstone but that's another story.)

You cannot miss the distinctive tower of St Andrew's. Rather bizarrely it has a gabled roof within the top of the tower. It would appear to be the only one in Norfolk although online church expert Simon Knott points to two in Suffolk; at Hepworth and Bromeswell.

Closer up, the north wall bears witness to a lost aisle – although it is unclear how long ago the demolition work took place. The nave is Norman while the solid-looking tower dates back to the 14th century. Finally look out for the substantial gravestone of John Pyke – the farmer behind Claxton's narrow gauge railway.

DIRECTIONS: St Andrew's is not on the Wherryman's Way proper but it is on Circular Walk 5.

The very remote St Peter's Church, Carleton.

Orimur Morimur: the five children of Mr Salletts.

St Peter's Church, Carleton

St Peter's Church sits in splendid isolation both from the tiny village it serves and just about everything else too. While many a Norfolk church sits a little aloof from the locals, St Peter's goes one better; refusing even to be at a roadside. Instead the visitor needs to walk across a ploughed field to reach the churchyard. The building dates back to Norman times although there could well have been a church on this site before that. Church specialist Simon Knott is a fan – not least because the building is always open.

"Here is a place where generations of pilgrims and strangers have been able to stop for a while, an ancient space in which to rest," he writes on his website.

"A little bit of England that still belongs to everybody. If the authorities start locking places like St Peter then it will be the end, and there won't be any point in celebrating such lovely, ordinary churches."

Hear, hear. Inside, notice the building's strange tunnel-like quality. It is because - very unusually – the church has a continuous nave and chancel.

On the north wall is a plaque commemorating "Mr Sallett's five children who lay interred in this holy place." According to the village history book Mr Sallett was the rector of the church between 1667 and 1699.

"Orimur morimur" translates as "We have risen and we have set."

DIRECTIONS: St Peter's is not on the Wherryman's Way, nor a circular walk. From Cramp Corner turn right towards Claxton and then first left up Ferry Road. The church is about a half a mile up this road on the right.

Buckenham Ferry and The Beauchamp Arms

The Beauchamp Arms might have been called The Beauchamp Arms for decades, but try telling that to the locals. To them it will always be called Buckenham Ferry, despite Buckenham being on the other side of the river and despite the long absence of any boat dedicated to taking you there. The bay for that ferry remains on our side of the river, while the last vestiges of a short jetty on the north side were removed as recently as 2007.

The Beauchamp Arms from the Buckenham bank.

With today's eyes it does not look a promising place for a ferryman plying for trade. A scattering of houses is visible on our side of the river, while only Buckenham station is obvious on the north bank. Yet this was a bustling junction when the writer P H Emerson arrived here for his 1893 book *On English Lagoons*.

"Day and night the ferry-bell was jangling and the winch clanking as the actors of country life passed before us in endless panorama," he wrote.

"Milk carts, carriers' carts, waggons laden with grain, flocks of sheep attended by shepherd and barking collies, stylish ladies in smart Norfolk carts…."

Once again the villages on either bank talked to each other in a way which has long-since been abandoned. Boatbuilder Paul Wright (see later in this chapter) remembers it from that era.

"I remember going across with my father in a lorry to take sugar beet to Cantley before the war," he recalled in April 2008.

All that remains of the ferry now is the bay where it once docked.

"And at one stage during the war the army put a pontoon bridge across."

The pub itself is named after the Proctor-Beauchamp family who owned large swathes of land on both sides of the river – including the Langley estate. The norfolkpubs website has found references back to 1704 when it was called "The Buckenham Ferry House".

The present building is more recent. Writing in 1951, James Wentworth Day said "the new house has taken the place of an older and far more picturesque inn which stood there in the old days".

Unlike some Wherryman's Way walkers who apparently pause here to use the outside loo without visiting the bar, Wentworth Day did the decent thing. He "drank a pint of ale in an austere bar which seemed to possess most of the features of Edwardian pub-house architecture. A pleasant landlady was, however, a compensation."

PEOPLE: *Cecil Nicholls*

Finding the date and the precise reason for the demise of the ferries along the river is a tricky business and Buckenham Ferry is no exception. Jack Points tried hard in his 1994 book Chain Ferries Over the Yare. He spoke to a number of retired farmers who could all remember its last years. The date narrowed to between 1938 to 1940 but he got no further.

Cecil Nicholls.

Which is why retired farm worker Cecil Nicholls is so important. He was born in Langley and now lives in Loddon. While a few people can remember using the ferry, Mr Nicholls is perhaps the only person left to have worked it too.

"We used to crank it across us boys," he told me. "If we were down there when a car turned up, the landlord would get us to do the work and we'd maybe get tuppence for
our trouble."

But even more remarkably Mr Nicholls can remember the precise day the ferry met its end.

"It was 1938 and we were all down at the pub for an agricultural workers presentation – there were lots of people there.

"Mr Lake from Claxton – I don't know his first name but we all called him 'Liney Lake' – came down there. He had seven tons of sugar beet on his lorry and he didn't put his handbrake on.

"The lorry went straight into the river, and that was it for the ferry. It was taken up to the Hardley blacksmith's shop and broken up."

Rowing boats remained for a while, but farmers had to find another way to transport their produce. Slowly the communities on either side of the river learned to ignore each other. And these days it is only octagenarians like Cecil Nicholls who can remember it any other way.

Paul Wright's boatyard

Tucked between The Beauchamp Arms on one side and Buckenham Sailing Club on the other, lies another less-heralded building.

It belongs to local boatbuilder Paul Wright, one of the pioneers of fibre-glass dinghies. For the last fifty years a host of different designs have been created here. A farmer's son, Mr Wright's love-affair with boats began when his father Gilbert took him on a hire cruiser before the war. Soon he had turned his hand to making his own boat on this very stretch of river.

Paul Wright.

Much later he started experimenting with a new-fangled material called fibre-glass – as well as gradually persuading his father that his future lay in a boatyard rather than a farmyard.

"It was obvious to me right from the beginning that fibre-glass had huge advantages over wood," he told me.

"With wood there is so much maintenance, with fibre-glass you can forget all that rubbing down and varnishing."

Soon he was building dinghies to sell. The Blue Streak was followed by the Silver Streak before he had the chance to build a fibre-glass version of the previously wooden-hulled Osprey.

But he enjoyed his greatest success with the Phantom, a single-handed high-performance sailing dinghy which he designed with Raveningham-based Brian Taylor in the early 1970s. His wife Myrtle still keeps the books on the Phantom design. During my visit in April 2008 boat number 1,319 had just been logged.

When demand eased for boats, Mr Wright experimented with other uses for his magic material. Fibre-glass greenhouses and swimming pool covers soon followed. Look carefully at the Starters Box on the Buckenham Sailing Club building. Yes, it too is made of fibre-glass.

Buckenham Sailing Club

Paul Wright's enthusiasm for boatbuilding lives on with the sailing club that he inspired. The people who bought his dinghies wanted somewhere to meet and race. And so – on October 2nd, 1959 – they set up Buckenham Sailing Club. Fifty years later it is still going strong with more than 80 members. And even today, Phantoms are an important part of the club's fleet.

"We may be in the middle of nowhere," said club commodore Simon Cullum.

"But as far as river sailing goes, this is the best bit of river there is. The tide makes it challenging, the big bends mean you get every aspect of sailing, we get good wind and there are very few trees."

The club holds races every Sunday from April through to December. Highlights include the Rockland Race around the broad - and the "Triple B", Buckenham to Breydon and Back. In my humble opinion you will struggle to find a friendlier sailing club anywhere on the Norfolk Broads.

Buckenham Sailing Club – complete with fibre-glass starter's box.

CIRCULAR WALK 5

DISTANCE: 5 miles

STARTS: Rockland Staithe car park

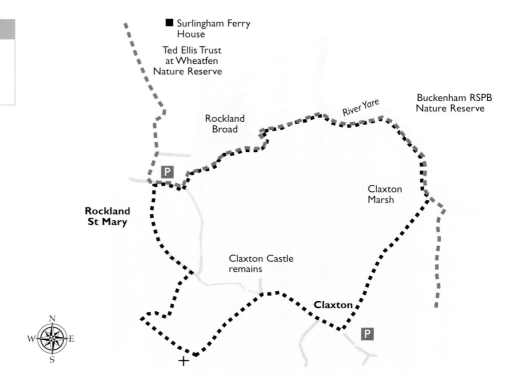

Surlingham Ferry House

Ted Ellis Trust at Wheatfen Nature Reserve

Rockland Broad

River Yare

Buckenham RSPB Nature Reserve

Rockland St Mary

Claxton Marsh

Claxton Castle remains

Claxton

N W E S

Circular Walk 5: Carleton Beck – with Beauchamp Arms in the distance.

DIRECTIONS: From Rockland Staithe take the Wherryman's Way path to the right of the dyke. Follow the path around first Rockland Broad and then Short Dyke to reach the Yare. Follow the river for about a mile, then turn right on a footpath just before you reach the Beauchamp Arms. This path runs alongside Carleton Beck and eventually emerges onto the main road in Claxton. Turn right and continue for about half a mile. Turn left onto a bridleway opposite Claxton Manor Farm. You might want to continue for just a few yards past the path to glimpse Claxton Castle in the grounds opposite.

Head uphill towards the distinctive tower of Claxton Church. Ignore the first footpath on the right, but take the second one through an arch in a hedge to emerge in the churchyard. Leave through the gate and cross the road onto another footpath next to a house. This path heads through fields with good views across the Yare Valley. Turn right onto a track which bends back towards Burton's Farm. Here, turn left onto the road. Cross a bridge over a stream and then turn left up a track. Stay to the left of a house and follow the stream through fields. At a "crossroads" on the edge of a field, turn right away from the stream up alongside a conifer plantation. You should see houses along a road in the distance. This is New Inn Hill. Turn right to return to the pub and the car park.

THE WHERRYMAN'S WAY - DIRECTIONS

This one's easy. In summary, stay next to the river until you get to the pub. Leave the pub by road and then turn left.

The pub avenue apart, notice how we are starting to lose the trees. The areas of green shading on the OS map become noticeably rarer downstream from Rockland Broad – at least on our side of the river. Looking across the Yare towards the horizon we can see the last significant woods on the north bank.

They form Buckenham Carrs, home to the small twin broads of Buckenham and Hassingham. They also provided the inspiration for the book *Crow Country*, written by author and naturalist Mark Cocker. Cocker sees the birds flying over his Claxton house and tracks down their roosting place. He finds the answer at Buckenham Carrs, where they gather in their tens of thousands.

From the Beauchamp Arms look out for the abandoned Buckenham Ferry Mill on the north bank.

Quoting everyone from the Roman poet Virgil to the New Wave Band XTC, *Crow Country* explores the corvid species from every conceivable angle. The experts call his book an "English pastoral classic". It is also a gentle love letter to the Yare Valley.

On the north bank we can also see Buckenham Halt – the tiny railway station beloved of birders who visit the nearby nature reserves. Coincidentally the halt is also the location for the beginning of another classic Wherryman's Way book – Black Sailed Traders. Author Roy Clark and old-time wherryman Jack Cates are taking a recently-restored wherry down the Yare with 40 tons of logs on board. *Albion* has been left moored at Buckenham when Clark joins as wherryman's mate. Clark was one of a select band who had helped save *Albion* in 1949. In just one chapter he simultaneously takes us on a voyage to Beccles and back in time; summoning the ghosts of wherries and wherrymen past.

The Wherryman's Way itself, meanwhile, continues along the Yare till first Carleton Beck and then The Beauchamp Arms. Once we cross the beck we are in Carleton St Peter. Ignore the beck footpath and continue to the pub. Then take the tree-lined and pot-holed avenue back to the road. This triangle is called Cramp Corner. Turn left here and continue along the road to Langley Green and Chapter 8.

Chapter 8 Langley with Hardley

"Oyez, oyez, oyez, if there be any manner of person that will absume, purfy, implead, or prosecute any action, suit, plaint or plea for any trespass or misdemeanour, done or committed upon the King's Majesty's river of Wensum, let him repair unto the Right Worshipful Mayor or the Worshipful Sheriff of the City of Norwich for the redress thereof and he shall be heard, God Save the King."

Proclamation which used to be made every year at Hardley Cross – the border between Norwich and Yarmouth's jurisdiction on the river. The Yare – it seems – used to be called the Wensum.

Langley Dyke.

"Bob Burgess was at the Round House and he could see it virtually hedge-hopping across Limpenhoe Marshes. The aircraft crashed into the wall of the Yare opposite Hardley Dyke and then Bob rowed round from the Round House to rescue him."

Mr Burgess lived there until 1957 when the giant Langley Hall Estate was split up at auction. Since then it has been a private house. Indeed on a windswept winter's day there can't be many houses more private, in the whole of Norfolk.

PEOPLE: *Anthony Ward*

Anthony Ward.

Anthony Ward was a teenager with a keen interest in local history during the Second World War. From his home in Norwich he would ride for miles visiting remote villages and bustling market towns.

Armed with little more than a fountain pen and a notebook, he wrote down what he heard and sketched what he saw.

"You'd just go and see what you could find," he told me.

"The fact that the war was on was a help really. These places were often deserted so you could do what you liked."

He was particularly fascinated by machinery and drainage systems. Many of the pumps draining the marshes were still powered by steam. All that was on the point of being swept away by first diesel, and then the electric pumps which survive to this day.

"No-one was interested in preserving mills and the like. And no-one else was talking to the marshmen who were still there."

But Mr Ward was – and he was just in time. At Monk's Loke – upriver from Langley Dyke so inaccessible to us – the building looked derelict. But inside, the boiler, the furnace and a rusty engine were still in place.

He tracked down "Loony" Crisp – a marshman in his 80s who had worked the engine in its glory days. Crucially Mr Ward wrote down Loony's memories in his own words:

"The boiler you scummed and blowed off every day," he told Mr Ward.

"Feedwater woz drawn from the deek [dike] and woz full of mud and the organic matter made a lot of scum. If you got the water level right you woz alright. Too low and you lorst a lot of steam but if it woz too high you lorst a lot a water an that wor worse."

"…Coal come up by sailing wherry, anything between 30 and 50 tons. Welsh steam coal woz the best for firing, but it woz a nuisance to handle because the lumps were so big. Sometimes you could only get one lump on a barrow. This woz a day's work for two men on the wherry and me."

There was enough there for Mr Ward to sketch reconstructions of how the steam mill would have looked in full working order.

continued…

Nothing survives of that building today, and nothing survives of Langley Roundhouse pump either. It was presumably somewhere near the site of today's electric pump. Mr Ward sketched a layout of that mill from remains he found there in 1961.

"This was arguably the finest of the Broads steam engines with an equally fine engine house," he wrote in an article for the Norfolk Industrial Archaeology Society.

"Now only a few piece of steel and road and overgrown bricks mark its passing."

But we know a lot more about it than we might – thanks to one enterprising teenager.

Anthony Ward's sketch of the Roundhouse mill.

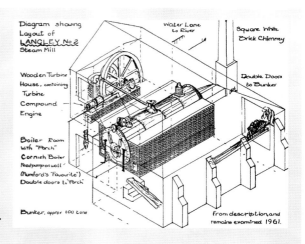

Diagram showing Layout of LANGLEY No 2 Steam Mill

Wooden Turbine House, containing Turbine Compound Engine

Water Lane to River

Square White Brick Chimney

Double Doors to Bunker

Boiler Room with "Porch" Cornish Boiler feedpump on wall (Mumford's 'Favourite') Double doors to Porch

Bunker, approx 100 tons

from description, and remains examined 1961.

Cantley: birthplace of the home-grown British sugar industry.

CANTLEY SUGAR FACTORY – FACTS

- Cantley was this country's first sugar beet factory. It was built in 1912.
- Sugar beet was delivered to the factory seasonally. The traditional "campaign" lasts from September through to February.
- In April 2009 the factory won planning permission to process beet throughout the year.
- Sugar is stored in six silos, each with a capacity of 10,000 tonnes.
- British Sugar supplies granulated sugar, caster sugar and a variety of other special types used as ingredients by the food industry.

Hardley Mill

At last our journey's first restored windmill. But Hardley Mill has only looked this good since the summer of 2009 when it was finally fitted with new sails.

For architect Peter Grix it was the culmination of almost a quarter of a century of effort. He had known the mill when he was a pupil at nearby Langley School. Decades later he returned on a family holiday and fell in love with it. But it was seven years before he was able to sign the lease which would allow him to begin restoration. In fact there was precious little to restore. Inside, only the main (vertical) drive shaft and a couple of floor beams survived.

Left: During the campaign, the factory works around the clock.

With a group of friends Mr Grix kept going; repairing the tower, removing its cap and making it weatherproof. He spent £100,000 of his own money but it was painfully slow work. Then in 2005 he formed the Friends of Hardley Windmill which quickly helped to spread the word locally. With the Wherryman's Way in existence, the mill felt slightly less out on a limb. Soon it attracted European money for a visitor centre and moorings as well as the restoration project itself. Professional millwrights were drafted in and on April 17th 2009 the local TV cameras were there to witness the mill's new cap gingerly being lowered into place by crane.

"You've got to be mad to do this sort of thing," said Peter, who left his wife in London while he restored the mill during the week.

"I've just got a passion for mills and am fascinated by their mechanisms. They are an extraordinary piece of machinery. It's terrible to see so many falling down in the Broads."

But the most extraordinary thing was the age of the people behind the hard graft of restoration. When it was finished last year, Rudolf Gunter from Cringleford was 83 while Michael Stephenson from Marsham near Aylsham was 71. Wally Gould from Bawburgh was 70 while David Battell from Hardley a mere baby at 57.

Peter adds: "What has knocked me out is the guys who have helped me. They are mainly OAPs and I never expected them to be driving miles, four days a week for two years, as reliable as clockwork, bringing enormous skills to unique problems. It's been great fun and hard work. That's what makes me proud."

The mill was built by millwright Dan England for the landowners the Proctor-Beauchamps. (The "TWBPB" stone inscription within the mill brickwork refers to Sir Thomas William Brograve Proctor-Beauchamp.) The Englands were famous for their turbine pump mills – considerably more powerful than the simple scoop wheel used by earlier mills. The so-called Appold turbine works using centrifugal force. Water is whipped up by an "impeller" and flung out at a higher level. At full pelt, it was capable of raising twelve tons of water per minute via a twelve-feet high vertical shaft.

Watertight: the first stage in the restoration of Hardley Mill.

Hardley Mill's demise

Local resident Cecil Nicholls can remember Hardley Mill's final night – he thinks it was 1947.

"I remember it had been a warm humid June day and I had been working at Avenue Farm drilling cabbages," he told me more than fifty years later.

"I got home about 4.30 and suddenly this storm started to brew up from nowhere. I've never seen thunder and lightning like it.

"A little while later my father came back and said the mill's sails had been wrenched off. The newspapers said they had been struck by lightning, but I think they were blown off."

Whatever the precise cause, those particular sails would never turn again. The mill was replaced by an electrical drainage pump, leaving the stump of the windmill to decay until Peter Grix stepped in to stop the rot.

Second stage: the cap goes on...

Third stage: complete with stocks...

Final stage: ...and sails.

Hardley Staithe

When the Yare was Norfolk's major artery for trade, Hardley was strategically placed. Never a big village, its short dyke nevertheless connected it to the main thoroughfare. Produce from the farms was shipped out, supplies of coal and timber could easily come in.

All that hard work meant there was a need for a pub right on the staithe. It seems to have been called The Staithe House during the first half of the 19th century and The Chequers in the second half. The norfolkpubs website dates its demise to 1896. It was far from being the only building here, there were barns and cottages too.

In contrast to Langley Dyke which has some free 24-hour moorings, Hardley is private. "Hardley Dyke No facilities Difficult to turn" is the distinctly unfriendly notice that greets boats at its junction with the Yare.

...Hardley Dyke.

St Margaret's Church

Sitting proudly on high ground, St Margaret's dominates the surrounding countryside.

You must be able to see for miles from the top of this venerable old tower. Certainly its castellated crest will pop up time and time again as we explore the Chet Valley.

Architecturally, it dates back to at least Norman times, with a makeover in the fifteenth century. The one later addition is a red-brick vestry from the nineteenth century, complete with an extravagant chimney. Inside, the church's decorations are in keeping with its role as surveyor of the marshes beyond. Look out for the wall painting of St Christopher – complete with willow, heron and fish.

There are also the scratched outlines of boats on the pews on the left-hand side of the church, presumably drawn by children during dull sermons.

Hardley Staithe in 1930.

ARCHIVE: *Hardley Cross*

With its protective fence and its lichen-encrusted stone work, Hardley Cross looks as if it belongs in the corner of a municipal park. Instead it stands alone at the confluence of the Rivers Chet and Yare; a tiny piece of man-made order amid a natural landscape of reed and river.

It's there because Hardley Cross used to mark the border of the jurisdictions of Norwich and Great Yarmouth. It might even have marked the western end of Breydon Water when the river was much bolder than it is today. So, unlikely as it may seem now, Hardley Cross was the scene of a major gathering of people once a year. The Mayor of Norwich and a substantial retinue came down the river, while the Mayor of Yarmouth came up, with a similarly large party.

Here the proclamation given in full at the beginning of the chapter would be read out. This was effectively an open-air court and it was used to clear the air between the two communities.

Hardley Cross.

Unlicensed traffic on the river would be dealt with, rows mediated, officials appointed. The cross itself could date back to the fourteenth or fifteenth century. County council experts say it is mentioned in a charter of 1556, while it appears to have been repaired in 1676, 1820 and 1899 among other occasions.

It remains in good condition today, providing another reminder of when the Yare was Norfolk's main thoroughfare, not a forgotten backwater.

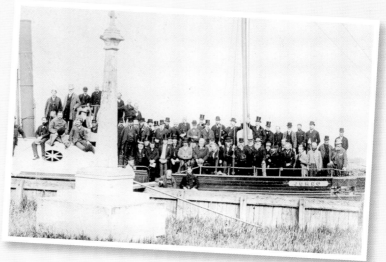

The great and the good at Hardley Cross in the 1880s.

Right: St Margaret's Church, Hardley.

Far right: Church graffiti.

Hardley Flood

Visit Hardley Flood at low tide when the wading birds come out to play and this stretch of water will slowly give up its secrets.

Strange shapes emerge from the shallows and it takes a while for the first-timer to realise that they are tree trunks – or rather the stumps of trees, and the ghosts of a previous landscape.

Because Hardley Flood is well-named. It used to be a mixture of grazing marsh and woodland, but it kept flooding. A long-running battle to try to keep it drained was finally lost during the floods of 1953. Ever since then "Hardley Marshes" have been replaced by Hardley Flood. The ranks of stumps used to be part of what old OS maps called Long Carr. Local resident Cecil Nicholls is one of the few who can remember this landscape before the flood.

A boardwalk alongside Hardley Flood.

Sunset on Hardley Flood.

"It was sixty acres of grazing marshes belonging to two farms," he remembered, "with carrs there as well."

"Some belonged to Dairy Farm which was called Lye's Heath farm in my day and the rest belonged to Hardley Hall farm. I can remember my dad delivering sacks of corn down a path from Lye's Heath farm to an old boathouse. All that path is under water now."

The farms survive with fewer fields, but somehow they seem insignificant in comparison to this magnificent stretch of water.

Hardley Flood has become home to important breeding populations of ducks like shoveller, pochard and gadwall. It has been designated a Site of Special Scientific Interest as a result.

Nature has reclaimed what humans once drained and most of us aren't complaining.

CIRCULAR WALK 6

DISTANCE: 7.5 miles

STARTS: Hardley Dyke

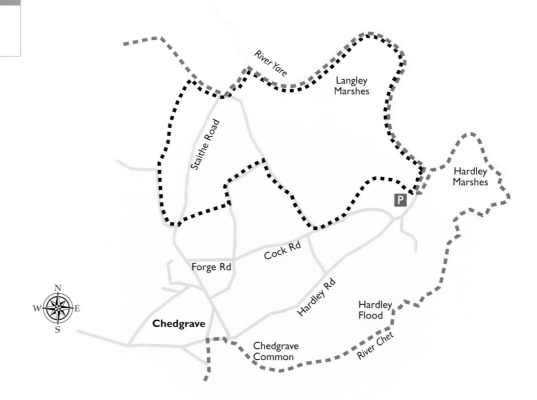

The "two village" sign.

DIRECTIONS FOR CIRCULAR WALK 6: Take the sign-posted footpath behind the end of the dyke and head along the edge of a field. You emerge onto a road with houses. This is Hardley Street. Follow the road past the houses for about half a mile. Take the first right turn, crossing a ditch called Guy's Gutter in the process. There are more houses on both sides of the road and a small green. Notice how the village sign is actually a two-village sign.

Continue along this road for another half a mile before turning left into Gentleman's Walk. Climb the hill and follow the road past some houses and around a sharp left-hand bend.

Turn right along a broad bridleway across fields to reach Staithe Road. Turn left and then immediately right down The Avenues, opposite some almshouses. The Avenues soon turns right past The Grange.

The footpath off to the left here takes you to Langley Church, well worth a two-minute detour. The church is very close to the grounds of the private Langley School. The school was previously the home of the Proctor Beauchamp family, the major landowner in these parts between the mid-18th and mid-20th century.

We continue along the road until it bears left where we take a narrow footpath straight on through a wood, passing alongside open water called Hazelmere Hole. Continue through a field, gently descending all the time. After this the path becomes more of a green lane and eventually emerges onto a road opposite smart flint cottages.

We turn right, soon passing the entrance to the Langley Abbey Estate, then the war memorial. Turn left down a footpath towards Langley Dyke, opposite the former Wherry pub.

We are now on the Wherryman's Way proper. Keep to the right of the dyke and walk down to the River Yare. Continue past The Round House (keeping on the raised path, and not straying into the house's front garden). The newly-restored Hardley Mill is next before our path turns right along Hardley Dyke and back to where we started.

THE WHERRYMAN'S WAY - DIRECTIONS

The Wherryman's Way in this chapter is dominated by a building on the other side of the river – the huge looming presence of the Cantley Sugar Works.

During the next six or seven miles we will see this industrial behemoth from just about every conceivable angle. Sometimes your nose will detect its sweet smell too.

Our route starts on the road from Claxton. We soon pass Monks Terrace, a group of former council houses designed by Herbert Tayler and David Green. Take a second look because Tayler and Green win plaudits from anyone who knows anything about architecture. Even the iconic Pevsner guide praises them. Their work here and in places like Loddon and Ditchingham was considered revolutionary in the 1950s.

Later we pass the Langley Abbey estate set back on the other side of the road. Continue straight on at the Langley war memorial road junction and then left down a footpath opposite the former Wherry pub. The wrought iron surround for the pub sign is still there – it just lacks its picture as the building lacks beer.

Stay to the right of this short dyke until you reach the Yare which quickly meanders left. That left turn leaves us staring straight down the barrel of the sugar works and its neighbour The Reedcutters pub – formerly the Red House.

The Reedcutters: tantalisingly out of reach.

To the right of our path – and the other side of a dyke – is a track which also runs all the way down to the river. Today the "Private" signs could not be more obvious, but older residents call this track "Loades Carnser". They say it was well-used by Langley people heading for Cantley Station, via yet another ferry. Cecil Nicholls, born in 1926, remembers two concrete posts with a bell in between.

"If you rang the bell the son of the people who ran the Red House would come out and row you across. You might have to use duckboards to get from the bell to the boat if it was high tide."

"I remember meeting people off the ferry late at night. The thing you didn't like was the rats running over your feet in the dark."

The Victorians reckoned these reaches of the Yare to be "the best for match sailing on the river". Writer George Christopher Davies said there were regular regattas here, while his contemporary Nicholas Everitt described Cantley as being almost "the headquarters of the Yare Sailing Club, which has for some time been the largest sailing club in the world..."

The sugar factory dominates the landscape.

On our side of the river the next building is the Round House. This is very much a private house. Its owners are understandably bemused when walkers decide to eat picnics on the table in their front garden.

Please stick to the path on the rond (the raised bank) and give them a bit of privacy.

Just downriver is the restored Hardley Mill, then the river twists again towards Hardley Dyke. At the landward end of Hardley Dyke you can cheat. The Wherryman's Way continues back along the other side of the dyke. If you are short of time, head up the road towards Hardley Church, turn left towards Hardley Hall and then left again along a track back to the Chet. Purists will continue back to the Yare, pass the derelict Limpenhoe Mill on the north bank and reach the confluence of the rivers Chet and Yare. Hardley Cross marks the spot.

We then wind our way tortuously along the Chet. Confusingly it sometimes looks as if you are heading back towards the ever-present sugar works. For some reason I find this the most God-forsaken part of the whole walk. Open skies and strange angles play tricks on you. It seems to take ages to get anywhere.

Everything changes once we reach the sanctuary of Hardley Carr and Hardley Flood. We are now on a narrow strip of land with the Chet on one side and the Flood on the other. Hardley Flood is simply one of the most under-rated spots in all of Norfolk, let alone the Wherryman's Way. Stay awhile if you can.

There is one stretch along this path where you can see both the round tower of St Margaret's Church in Hardley on your right and the octagonal tower of St Gregory's, Heckingham on your left. We were a few hundred yards from St Margaret's at Hardley Staithe and later we will walk directly alongside St Gregory's en route to Reedham Ferry. They are about a mile apart as the crow flies but we will walk at least eight miles in between.

We leave Hardley Flood behind and reach Chedgrave Common and Chapter 9.

Chapter 9 Loddon and Chedgrave

"I would encourage everyone who can do so to make the voyage; for Loddon is, to my mind, a very charming little place, and a saunter through it, a game of bowls on the old green at the back of the Swan Inn …a visit to the church and then Chedgrave Church are a sufficient recompense for any difficulty which may be encountered on the river."

William Dutt, The Norfolk Broads 1903

Loddon Staithe.

Afte a succession of villages the small town of Loddon and its sidekick village Chedgrave feel almost metropolitan.

If you are walking the Wherryman's Way in two days this is undoubtedly the place to break your journey. Not only are there two Bed and Breakfasts, there are also pubs, shops, takeaways and a Bangladeshi restaurant. The two places grew up quite separately. Loddon was much bigger – the classic small market town. Until very recently Chedgrave was tiny in comparison.

In the past Loddon was also the headquarters for the local council. Today it still feels like an unofficial capital for this part of Norfolk. Chedgrave too has expanded rapidly in the last three or four decades.

Those extra residents have helped ensure the survival of a busy high street. Holidaymakers on hire boats used to be big business here too. Demand has waned, but Loddon Staithe can still fill up quickly on a sunny summer weekend.

Finally the history of both Loddon and Chedgrave has been well-documented by local historians Christina Crease and Carol Carpenter. Many thanks to them for allowing me to use their extensive archive at Loddon Library.

Loddon: almost metropolitan.

The noble Saxon lord Aelfric Modercope welcomes you to Loddon. The first written mention of Loddon comes in his will.

The River Chet

The view of the River Chet from Loddon Staithe looks timeless enough. Yet both the course and the scope of the river have changed dramatically over the years. Take Loddon Mill for example. The timber-framed building was built in either the late 17th century or the early 18th century.

The Wherry Hathor leaves Loddon.

Quanting: back-breaking work.

Above: Digging out a deeper Chet for the wherries.

Right: Loddon Staithe: previously not so pretty.

Loddon Staithe marks the head of navigation on the Chet.

It was built some 50 yards south of the river; the waters were diverted to run underneath it. The Chet's previous course would have cut across today's allotments.

Further downstream too, man has meddled. Christina Crease and Carol Carpenter have established that much of the present river between the staithe and Pyes Mill was deepened and straightened by manual labour at the turn of the last century. The original course was slightly further north – the Chedgrave side.

The work was paid for by two corn and seed companies who wanted to make the Chet navigable for their wherries. You can read about one of those merchants – Woods, Sadd, Moore and Company – at the staithe itself. So what today could be considered a beauty spot, was for many decades rather industrial, if not downright ugly. The last vestiges of that era were swept away as recently as 1970.

The Chet begins its life just to the west of Poringland. The ground there rises to 70 metres above sea level – radar and radio aerials mark the spot. On one side of these hills the streams run west into the Tas Valley. On the other, a tiny Chet starts its dozen-or-so mile run down to the River Yare at Hardley Cross.

Tracking the youthful Chet is no easy business, but local people agree that its source lies somewhere close to Poringland Community Wood on Carr Lane. A few hundred yards south of there, it used to snake diagonally across a field to the north of Howe Lane. Retired builder David Dicks remembers going "sticklebacking" along this stretch as a boy in the 1940s. By the 1960s all that had changed. Farmer Roger

Kidner decided to pipe the Chet underground. Two irregular-shaped fields became one more manageable area as a result.

So now the first we see of the Chet, is as a tiny ford on Howe Lane in Poringland. From there it follows Dove Lane and – according to Ordnance Survey – becomes the "Well Beck" as it heads east between Alpington and Brooke.

The OS finally admits it is the Chet at Busseybridge Farm in Bergh Apton – and indeed it gives that parish its southern boundary. Growing bolder by the mile it then arcs round the beautiful wood of Sisland Carr en route to Loddon.

ARCHIVE: *Loddon Mill*

From a corn mill powered by water to a well being centre for complementary therapy, the history of Loddon Mill tells us quite a lot about our ever-changing priorities.

In between times, this building has also been powered by steam and electricity as well as seeing later incarnations as a restaurant and a furniture showroom. Throughout it all, its weather-boarded frontage has provided an elegant gateway to Loddon by road and river.

Today it is split into three dwellings. To the right – as seen from the road – is the well-being centre. The central higher section is one property, while the left hand side would originally have provided a home for the miller. The Mill House now also includes the empty engine room and truncated chimney from the mill's steam days.

Loddon Mill.

The mill itself finally stopped working in 1968. According to present owners Andy and Katherine Walter, the engine room remained virtually untouched until they bought the house. Both work in the music industry. So when they had finished restoring it in 2008 they were able to arrange a charity concert there featuring an internationally-renowned quartet. It is yet another chapter in the ever-changing life of this landmark building.

Loddon Mill – the chimney was for a steam engine which provided extra power for the mill.

PEOPLE: *Caroline Dwen*

Caroline Dwen has seen thousands of Wherryman's Way walkers troop through her tiny Rosy Lee's tearoom in Loddon. Resistance is futile. You will sit down. You will enjoy tea in china cups. You will fall for her infectious enthusiasm.

"The Wherryman's Way is the best thing to have happened to Loddon for both tourists and locals," she says.

"It's good for the shops, the pubs as well as for people's health and the environment. They all pass through here on their way. Lots of them start here too … some head for Norwich, others to Yarmouth."

Rosy Lee's started in 1999 with a second-hand fridge, a table sawn in two and teapots from charity shops. In truth, not much has changed since – except that the choice of food has steadily become more ambitious and it has also become an informal gallery for local artists' work.

The tea room is also much busier. So much so that some say Caroline should move to bigger premises. But that would ruin the café's intimate feel. You simply can't ignore other people here, and that creates the friendly atmosphere which means people keep coming back.

Caroline Dwen: infectious enthusiasm.

All Saints Church Chedgrave

Architecturally, most people are rude about All Saints Church, Chedgrave. A twelfth century shell had what the Pevsner architectural guide calls "a frightful brick North aisle" added to it in the nineteenth century. Another brick extension was added in the 1990s. The guide describes that as being "like a two-storeyed house hitting one in the face". Congregation-wise it is a different story. There is a vibrant community here which regularly uses the church and both floors of the extension simultaneously as part of an innovative approach to attracting families back into church.

Left: All Saints Church, Chedgrave and right in 1907.

The Chet boatyards

There is something unusual along the banks of the Chet at Loddon – people at work. The coal sheds and the warehouses of the Victorian era might be long gone, but they have been replaced by boatyards and boatsheds, mostly dating from the 1950s and 1960s.

Dennis Walklin – born in 1935 – is now the grand old man of this watery industrial estate, having arrived in 1969.

"I sold my central heating business in Essex and bought a derelict boatyard instead," he told me.

"It sounds a bit crazy, but it was really quite exciting, even though at the time I knew nothing about boats."

He soon learnt, even though it was tough to start with. With limited money, he lived in a cement shed on site for the first three years while his wife and daughter stayed with her parents in Great Yarmouth. Work at the Cantley sugar factory supplemented his initially meagre takings. Steadily he built up a fleet of six boats at a time when a holiday on the Broads was becoming increasingly popular.

"If it floated you could hire it," he said.

"They were the golden years. Everyone used to come down here – even the stars. Cliff Richard would take a boat out on the Broads."

Boatyards exist on both sides of the river.

Mr Walklin pulled out of hire boats in 1987. Ten years later near neighbours Greenway Marine took the same decision. By then it was clear that the golden era was long gone; replaced for many by cheap holidays abroad. But businesses along this quiet stretch have diversified and still prosper. Fewer people hired boats, but more people bought them. They needed places to moor, places for boats to be laid up for the winter; people to repair them. The Chet boatyards have been happy to oblige.

Greenway has also branched out. Jonathan Greenway designed the "barrow boat" – a traditional clinker-built dinghy. The fixed wheel beneath the bow means it does not need a trolley and it has sold in its thousands.

Meanwhile Pacific Cruisers continue to fly the flag for the hire boat industry. Owners Richard and Fiona Husband started off ten years ago. They say there is still a market out there – especially among nature-lovers and anglers.

"Expectations have changed," said Fiona.

"People do want luxuries and we have to explain that no you won't be able to plug in your hair-straighteners. But we have our regular customers who simply love the peace and quiet of the Broads."

… And those customers probably love the traditional family-run boatyards too.

Parravani's ice cream

If you hear the tinkle of an ice cream van along the Wherryman's Way, the chances are it is owned by Chedgrave-based Parravani's.

Parravani's: purveyors of ice cream since 1898.

Guiseppe Parravani came to Britain in the footsteps of his brother, who had already set up an ice cream business in Norwich. By 1898 Guiseppe had saved up enough money to buy a cart of his own. He started to sell ice creams in villages around Bungay.

A wife and 11 children followed. Each one was recruited into the family business. They sold ice creams in the villages around Bungay – the joke being that the ponies would teach them the rounds.

Guiseppe's eldest son Agostino took over on his father's death in 1931 and retired in 1985. That meant that in 1986 for the first time in 88 years, no Parravani's ice cream was produced. This, goes the story, caused an outcry from the locals.

In response Agostino's brothers Dominic and Peter took over, soon handing the reins over to Dominic's son Paul who today runs the business with his wife Sharon from their base in Chedgrave. "These days the wholesale trade is the big growth area," Paul told me. "We sell a lot of ice cream to restaurants and hotels."

"And as well as ice creams and sorbets we also do home-made cakes and patisseries."

Hiring reliable people to drive the vans has become increasingly difficult in recent years. But they still have a fleet of six vehicles and two trailers. In many places the vans are doing the same rounds as the ponies and carts did years ago. They stop at the same places and in some cases they are now serving the fifth generation of their original customers.

The Pubs of Loddon and Chedgrave

The Swan

Historically, very much a grand coaching inn – you can still see the old stables at the back. The main building looks 18th century but an older timber-frame lurks beneath its brick façade. Receptions and dances used to be held here. Even the local magistrates used its rooms for their fortnightly "Petty Sessions". A bowling green survives to the rear. It made a great impression on the Edwardian writer William Dutt.

"Business seems to be practised during the day as a preliminary pastime to that resorted to every evening on the Swan bowling green, where the tradesmen meet in friendly rivalry as long as daylight lasts."

Loddon was granted a charter to hold a market in the mid-13th century and there was still a thriving "Sale Ground" behind The Swan until twenty-odd years ago. Today the yard between the pub and the green still plays host to a small weekly market.

The King's Head

Bridge Street used to be full of pubs, but now only The King's Head survives. The Jolly Farmers was on the site of Pennington's Opticians while the Red Lion was almost directly opposite The King's Head. Another pub called The Crown was also nearby.

The King's Head is probably the oldest of Loddon's three pubs. There is a small beer garden to the rear, next to a track down to a boatyard.

The Angel

They used to say that the workmen who built Holy Trinity Church in the 15th century used to enjoy a beer here, but Loddon's historians disagree. They say it is more likely to date from the 18th century. The Angel also has a beer garden, this time hidden behind outbuildings.

The White Horse

Chedgrave's only pub. The White Horse also boasts a bowling green and a beer garden. The pub has been recently renovated and now includes a restaurant.

Holy Trinity church

Most of the churches we have passed so far have been the work of many generations over many centuries. A Norman tower with a 13th century nave and a 15th century aisle, say. Look carefully and the different styles from those different eras will emerge.

But Holy Trinity at Loddon is different. The vast majority of it was built over the course of one generation and with the money of one man – Sir James Hobart. Sir James had become the Attorney General to Henry VII in 1486 – a year after the king had come to the throne.

Holy Trinity Church, Loddon.

You can see a picture of Sir James and his wife Margaret on the wall of the south aisle. Some say the work was completed within just a few years – some time within Henry VII's reign – 1485 to 1509.

Holy Trinity is also much bigger than anything we have encountered so far. St Mary's at Surlingham and St Peter's at Carleton are both older and smaller for example; very much village churches. The doughty dressed flint and confident Perpendicular windows here are impressively substantial in comparison.

Inside too, its dimensions impress. The church guide is spot-on: "On entering the nave, one's eyes fly upwards …to the great height of the hammer-beam roof and the clerestory windows – fifteen on either side."

Perhaps the most moving of many memorials in the church is also one of the most recent. Half way down the north aisle is a bas –relief tablet remembering two brothers. As the inscriptions make clear, both France and William Cadge from Loddon were killed within six months of each other during the First World War; one at Gallipoli the other at the Battle of Loos.

Brothers in Arms.

CIRCULAR WALKS

There are twelve circular walks based around the Wherryman's Way; four of those fall within this chapter.

CIRCULAR WALK 7

DISTANCE: 4.5 miles (7.5 miles longer route)

STARTS: Chedgrave Church

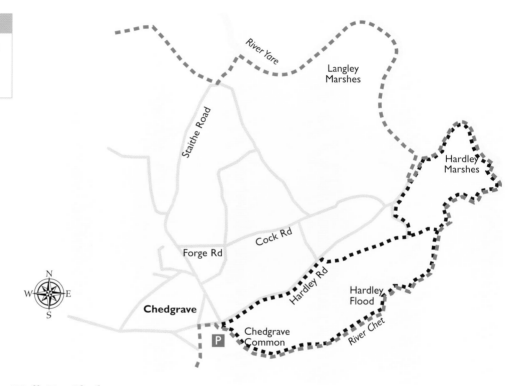

Circular Walk 7 – Sunset near Hardley Flood.

Walk 7 – Chedgrave

Walk through the Pits playground, turning right onto Pits Lane which descends towards the River Chet. Go through the gate to start following the river towards the Yare. The easy access path here runs as far as Chedgrave Common. A little further, the path reaches Hardley Flood – complete with bird hide.

Continue along the river bank past the Flood, past a private entrance to Hardley Hall and through a gate. At the second gate turn left along a track which overlooks Hardley Hall. This bridleway eventually hits the Hardley Road at its junction with Cross Stone Road. Turn left and walk back into Chedgrave passing the base for Parravani's Ice Cream on your left.

Alternatively continue along the river bank to the confluence of the Rivers Chet and Yare at Hardley Cross. From there continue around to Hardley Dyke. Walk up the road and take the left-hand turn onto Hardley Hall Lane. Take a right turn off here just before Hardley Hall onto the bridleway described above.

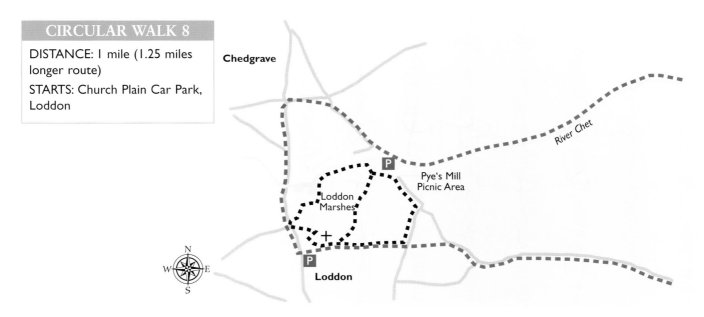

CIRCULAR WALK 8

DISTANCE: 1 mile (1.25 miles longer route)

STARTS: Church Plain Car Park, Loddon

Walk 8 – Loddon

Walk through Holy Trinity's huge graveyard heading down hill along a footpath to a bridge over a small stream called The Run.

Turn left when you reach a road – Mill Road. Head downhill and turn left at the t-junction into Pye's Mill Road. Pye's Mill used to be on the land between these two roads. These days Pye's Mill refers to the picnic spot at the end of Pye's Mill Road, next to the River Chet.

The road used to continue across the river to Chedgrave. An 1826 map of Norfolk shows "Pyes Mills Ford" here, complete with roads on either side.

Turn left and cross another bridge across the Run onto grazing marshes. You can either head back diagonally across the field to the church or hug the river. If you choose the latter you cross an often-boggy field to emerge next to a footbridge. A path from here heads back to Loddon High Street.

Circular Walk 8 – Pyes Mill.

CIRCULAR WALK 9

DISTANCE: 4 miles
STARTS: Church Plain Car Park, Loddon

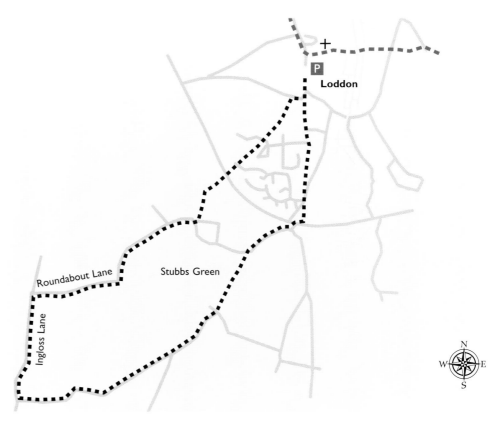

Loddon

Circular Walk 9 – to Bush Farm.

Walk 9 Loddon Ingloss

Turn left up the High Street soon passing The Angel pub on your left. Then stay to the right of the triangular Farthing Green and to the left of the butchers and walk the length of High Bungay Road.

Cross the staggered crossroads on the busy A146 Loddon bypass and then turn immediately right into Stubbs Green Lane. Bear left onto a track with two "5mph" signs and then take a footpath on your right onto a meadow called Stubbs Green Common Land.

You emerge onto a drive leading to Elm Farm – complete with its ramshackle barn. Continue straight ahead on a narrow road following a sign to Bush Farm. Pass Elm Cottage on your right and then take a footpath on the right across a field.

Continue to the edge of the field and then cross a track and a tiny bridge. This path takes you down alongside a hedge. At the end of the field turn left onto a path down to Ingloss Lane.

Turn right and walk along the road for half a mile. Then turn right again onto a green lane, marked only by a Wherryman's Way badge on a telegraph pole.

This is Roundabout Lane. It turns left along a hedge. Ignore other left turns until you hit woodland. Keep left at the fork and then left to enter a field which heads back towards the A146. Cross the road into a housing estate. Go straight down Alfric Close, then take a footpath on the left. Continue on this footpath which crosses a road and then passes Hobart High School. Turn right onto Kittens Lane and then left at the butchers to return to the car park.

Church Plain from the church tower.

Circular Walk 10 – on Warren Hills.

CIRCULAR WALK 10

DISTANCE: 5 miles

STARTS: Church Plain Car Park, Loddon

Walk 10 Loddon Warren Hills

Turn left up the High Street passing The Angel pub. Keep to the left of Farthing Green and follow the road through Loddon. Look out for the Fox and Hounds house on the right hand side. Until the mid-1990s this was the Fox and Hounds pub. Turn right along a footpath immediately after crossing a small stream called The Run.

Cross the A146 and go through the kissing gate across a sloping meadow known as Warren Hills. Pass through a chain gate and turn left up a path. At the end turn right onto a farm road passing Loddon Hall on your left. Turn right at the t-junction onto Transport Lane.

Turn left at the Kirby Cane Hall Farm info board and follow the farm track. Don't take the path to Hales Hall. Turn right at a track t-junction and keep to the right of a disused barn. A little further our route turns right to return towards Transport Lane. Turn right onto Transport Lane and then left over a footbridge. This path takes you back to Warren Hills.

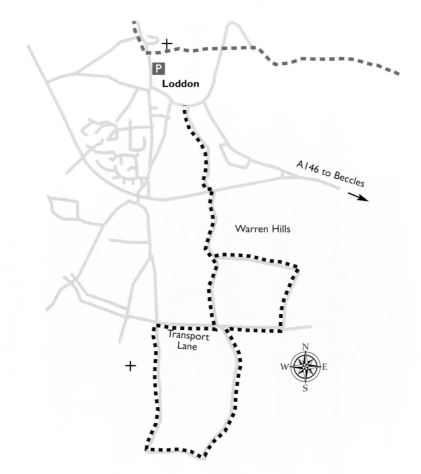

THE WHERRYMAN'S WAY - DIRECTIONS

From Chedgrave Common we continue to follow the Chet. The first signs of both Loddon and Chedgrave soon emerge in the distance on either side of the river. Pass through a gate and keep right, heading away from the river and the boatyards.

This ancient road heads gently uphill, passing houses new and old. We turn left into a beautiful playground set in a hollow, known as Chedgrave Pits. All Saints Church looks down from on high. The path emerges onto a road which quickly heads down to a crossroads, complete with a range of shops. Turn left here and continue to a junction with a main road.

Walk round the oak tree next to the post box. A plaque proudly proclaims it to be one of "50 Great British Trees in recognition of its place in the National Heritage". It was planted to mark the golden jubilee of Queen Victoria on June 21st, 1887. After drinks at the White Horse pub opposite, head towards Loddon. This road crosses a bridge which marks the head of navigation for the River Chet.

Once over the river we are in Bridge Street which becomes Church Plain, home to many of Loddon's prettiest houses as well as Holy Trinity Church. The steep gabled flint building on Church Plain used to be a school and is now a much-loved library. We walk to the far side of the Church Plain car park and turn left towards Holy Trinity's spacious graveyard. The path heads past the church and down towards a bridge over a small stream known as The Run. This is a perfect spot for playing pooh-sticks.

We continue up between private gardens, crossing Mill Road onto another path which emerges onto a meadow. Pass through an ancient kissing gate on the far side of the meadow and turn right onto a narrow road. Turn left at the crossroads to head onto Chapter 10 and Heckingham.

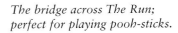

The bridge across The Run; perfect for playing pooh-sticks.

Chapter 10 Heckingham and Nogdam End

"Reedham Ferry could tell a good many tales of the cargoes of smuggled goods which used to be run across the marshes in the old days when the defunct Cockatrice Inn on the opposite bank, now a respectable farm house, was a notorious store house and changing place for cargoes of spirits, tobacco and other 'free trade' goods."
Broadland Adventure, James Wentworth Day, 1951

Dawn on the Chet near Norton Marsh Mill.

If Loddon got too busy, the next leg of our journey will make up for it. Heckingham is spread thinly across many acres, while Nogdam End is no more than a hamlet around a t-junction.

Though it is not entirely obvious to start with, we are slowly making our way back towards the River Yare along the south side of the Chet Valley. Most of our route is along roads – although the lanes are narrow and the traffic sporadic.

The one footpath takes us alongside the isolated St Gregory's Church. Why is it there? Because archaeological evidence suggests that Heckingham was much more substantial in earlier times.

St Gregory's Church and below.

Relics from the Stone, Iron and Bronze ages have been found here. And according to archaeologist Alan Davison, Heckingham was as big as Loddon when the Domesday Book was compiled in 1086. Rather mysteriously, it slowly shrank over the next two hundred and fifty years. More recently the village was known as the site of the notorious Heckingham workhouse – even if the building itself was much closer to the neighbouring village of Hales.

"The disorder and turbulence of the inmates were such as to triumph over the authority of the governor," wrote a Poor Law Commissioner in 1836.

Sundays, he said, were particularly lawless.

"It was found profitable to erect two beer-shops in the immediate neighbourhood, which were usually crowded with paupers. The women had boxes in the neighbouring cottages containing dresses, which … they exchanged for the workhouse garb, and thus attired in a more attractive style, flaunted about the neighbourhood in the company with the young men."

The bad news is that the last conventional pub along our route closed almost eighty years ago. The good news is that the next pub is just across the river at Reedham Ferry.

St Gregory's Church

This is quite the most beautiful, peaceful, perfect church along the entire Wherryman's Way. And it is perfect in some very Norfolk ways.

First, its position. It is spectacularly isolated; off a track, off a road in the middle of nowhere. But that reminds us of the transience of the population in these parts. Remember Heckingham used to be a much bigger settlement than it is today. Second there is the Norman doorway. Norfolk has an incredible number of churches which date back to Norman times. But the workmanship here – and at Heckingham's "twin" church of Hales – is extraordinary.

Third it is always open and always peaceful. I defy anyone to sit for five minutes in silence here and not come out feeling better for it. Fourth, there is the gruesome reality of the grinning skull motif on the tombstones inside the church. They feel insensitive to modern eyes and seem to survive only in churches off the beaten track.

Finally, do not leave St Gregory's graveyard without finding the broken pillar commemorating Dr Lawson Tait McClintock. Local historian Christina Crease has established that Dr McClintock was the local medical officer for Loddon during the First World War. He ran a Red Cross hospital in the lecture hall in George Lane. The hospital caught fire in October 1918. Despite suffering from flu, Dr McClintock got up to find new beds for his patients. As a result he developed complications, and died on 11th November 1918 aged 39. Why half a pillar? Because – they say – he only lived half a life.

Part of St Gregory's beautiful south doorway.

The grinning skull motif is still found in remote churches.

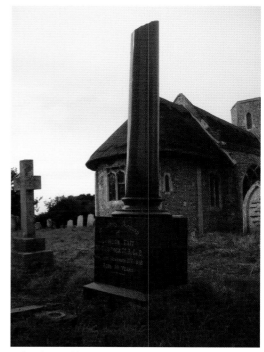

A broken pillar "in memory of half a life lived".

PEOPLE – *Mike Saunders*

One winter's morning in 1991, Essex businessman Mike Saunders got on a tube train at Upminster.

Short of something to read, he picked up a discarded property supplement. Among the three-bed semis, there was a derelict Norfolk windmill up for auction. Looking at the date, Mr Saunders realised he was too late; the auction had come and gone and he had surely missed out on a life-time's ambition to own a holiday home on the Broads.

"But something made me give them a ring to find out how much it went for," he said. "I was just curious."

That call changed everything. The auctioneer told him that Norton Marsh Mill had not found a buyer. Mr Saunders seized his chance. He closed the deal and quickly won planning permission to convert it into a holiday home.

Crucially he had to keep it traditional. The mill was given a traditional "Norfolk cap". A replacement scoop wheel cover was made using the rotting remains of the original as a template; even the dyke leading up to the mill was dug out to its original width.

"That tube train ride, well it just has to be fate doesn't it?" he said.

"Now it's our Norfolk home and we love it. Sometimes I'll just come out and sit on the bench here with a glass of wine at midnight watching the water go by. It's a very special place."

Norton Marsh Mill was probably built in 1863 and apparently decommissioned in 1917. Presumably it had declined and decayed slowly for much of the twentieth century. Now though it has a busy new life as a holiday home on four levels with tourists loving its 360 degree views.

….Something you cannot always guarantee on the tube at Upminster.

Norton Marsh Mill; beautifully restored.

Mike Saunders in 1997 with work well underway.

Old Hall Carr

There is a mystery lurking within the shaded acres of Old Hall Carr – and the clue is in the name.

Today's OS map reveals there is a moat inside the woods. So was there once a grand old building – an Old Hall – surrounded by protective water? Well, we think so, but we have precious little evidence. The earliest document – from 1697 – calls it "Beans Tenement". This talks rather vaguely about buildings and fishponds.

The first edition of the Ordnance Survey misspells it as "Old Hall Car" while the 1905 edition tantalisingly says "Old Hall – site of".

Today the land is owned by the Raveningham Estate. Estate archivist Dr Barbara Linsley says the moat was re-dug by German prisoners during the First World War. There had also been a small keeper's cottage house elsewhere in the wood, but that was demolished in 1983. Of the original Old Hall, we seem destined to know very little.

The Cockatrice

With an intriguing name and a desolate location, it is no wonder that the Cockatrice Inn always had something of an aura about it.

Today the building is a whitewashed house – the only house on the road which runs between Nogdam End and Reedham Ferry.

Formerly The Cockatrice pub, now a private house.

There was a pub because there was a staithe. Norton Staithe was once important enough to have barns and storehouses for the wherries' cargoes of coal and corn.

When the Broads writer Arthur Patterson passed The Cockatrice in 1930 there was:

"one wherry at its staithe, where a score or more were at one time keen to moor when thirsty. The day hath long passed when smugglers crept-to and landed at the staithe at night and the "Breydon Pirate" is all but extinct."

Patterson only just made it. According to today's owner Pamela Blinkhorn, The Cockatrice ceased to be a pub in 1931. But local people remember that it continued to look like a pub for many years afterwards.

"My grandparents lived there for 20 or 30 years until perhaps the late 1960s," said Trisha Betts who still lives nearby.

"I remember that one room in the building was always called The Bar, and the long bar itself was still there. There was just a load of old junk in there, my grandfather didn't change anything at all.

"I can remember wherries coming up to the staithe to pick up sugar beet ... and I can remember the barns there too."

"And there was certainly a slaughterhouse, because my grandmother was the first woman to have a slaughterer's licence."

But of course the days of smuggling along this desolate stretch are long gone. Or are they? One Nogdam End resident I spoke to swears otherwise. He says he has seen fast boats roar up this section of the Yare late at night …followed by mysterious lorries rumbling off into the distance. Details were scarce and he was keen to remain anonymous, but I wonder….

THE WHERRYMAN'S WAY - DIRECTIONS

We turned left at the crossroads at the end of Chapter 9 onto Norton Road. Continue along this lane until a track turns left towards Riverside Farm.

Just after the track, we turn left diagonally across a field in the direction of some houses nestling in a hollow. This is Heckingham Holes – a narrow lane which heads down towards Loddon Common, close to the River Chet. Loddon Common is the last parcel of land to still be owned by an ancient charitable body called the Loddon Town Estate. We turn left onto the lane and then almost immediately right onto a footpath before a white dutch-gabled building called The Wheel House. This path heads between gardens onto open country. Turn left at the first gate heading down into a field which is invariably marshy.

From here – in winter at least – you should be able to make out the octagonal top of St Gregory's church tower. Cross a stile-cum-bridge to emerge on a broad path next to the church itself. Follow the lane as it heads uphill to rejoin Norton Road. We turn left and then left again onto Ferry Road with magnificent views across to Hardley Flood.

After about half a mile the road takes a sharp right-hander to avoid Old Hall Carr on our left. Later, keep straight on as first one then another road join from the right. The second of these junctions is Nogdam End. The road now runs ruler-straight, passing a winding River Chet, then Norton Drainage Mill and the former Cockatrice pub. As the Chet brushes the road you can see Hardley Cross in the distance. Finally the road rubs up against the bank next to the Yare itself before we reach Reedham Ferry.

Heading for Heckingham Holes.

Philosophy on a bench.

Far left: All quiet at Nogdam End.

Left: Look out for Hardley Cross as you head to Reedham Ferry.

Chapter 11 Reedham

"The next day they sailed down the Waveney until they came to Haddiscoe, and then, instead of continuing down to Breydon Water, they went along the New Cut, a wide channel which unites the Waveney with the Yare, joining the latter at Reedham. They found the channel of the Yare very much broader than the Bure or the Waveney; and as they had a favourable breeze for the greater part of the way, and there was plenty of room to tack in the reaches where it was against them, they made rapid progress."

The Swan and her Crew, G. Christopher Davies, 1876

The Riverside at Reedham.

They say Reedham was the site of a Roman lighthouse and the seat of Saxon kings. It even has its own grisly legend involving a murdering huntsman and vengeful Danes – of which more later.

The lighthouse or pharos was here because Reedham would have been on the coast in Roman times. It is the only high ground for miles. Look east across the flat Halvergate marshes and it is easy to imagine the higher sea levels. Evidence for the pharos itself is limited, but you can certainly see Roman tiles within the walls in the village church.

While the sea might have retreated, the river is still significant. Indeed from Reedham Quay it feels as if every house looks down onto the Yare. In the nineteenth century Reedham was a centre for boatbuilding. Many fine wherries started life here – witness the statue of a boatbuilder on the river bank.

The other industry to have left its mark is the railway. It arrived in Reedham in 1844 as part of the Norwich to Great Yarmouth line. Later a second track joined it from Lowestoft by way of a swing bridge near The Ship pub. A wider swing bridge still operates to this day; its noiseless Open Sesame allowing yachts through.

Much of this history is summed up in the intricate village sign which includes images of the pharos and a Viking ship. It also depicts a newly-built wherry – identified as such because its sail has yet to be tarred black. The woman on the sign is Margaret Paston who became famous for the fifteenth century Paston letters. Finally Reedham is known for its chain ferry. This loveable old workhorse is now the only one of its kind on the Broads.

Reedham Ferry

So far on our journey down the Yare we have come across former ferries at a variety of locations in Norwich, Whitlingham, Bramerton, Surlingham, Buckenham and Langley. But it is only at Reedham that we can finally use the present tense.

Against all the odds, Reedham Ferry still exists, thrives even. Complete with 236 feet of chain, two diesel engines and hydraulically-operated loading ramps, it is the latest in a long line of boats to have carried vehicles and passengers safely across the river.

No-one knows how long there has been a ferry here. Author Jack Points tracked down a document signed in 1864 by a former pub landlord Jeremiah Hoggett. He said that his father had collected "tolls and dues at the ferry between 1773 and 1803, having succeeded

Reedham Ferry in the 1950s.

Reedham Ferry.

John Shepherd". That could easily take us back to the mid-18th century, but a ferry service of some kind may date back considerably further.

In the late 1940s it was praised in a *Country Life* article as being "the last of the Norfolk Horse Ferries" by prolific Broads writer James Wentworth Day.

"On the Yare, Buckenham and Surlingham Ferries have gone," he wrote.

"Yet half a century ago the black hulls and white-painted rails of the great, floating, box-like ferries with their cargoes of farm wagons, farmer's gigs, market carts and the village carrier's cart were as much a part of the peaceful rural scene as were the pink sun-bonnets of the marshwomen and the felt wide-awake hats of the marshmen."

At that time the landlord was Arthur Benns. His chain ferry dated back to 1924 and was operated by a hand winch.

"Arthur Benns, although past his seventieth birthday, thinks nothing of cranking 20 or 30 tons of dead weight across the river, sometimes with the tide running strongly and an easterly wind off the marshes cutting like a razor."

Wentworth Day caught the end of an era. Soon afterwards both ferry and pub were taken over by Norman Archer. Within a couple of years Mr Archer had replaced the hand winch with an engine.

"Our work is certainly much easier," he told the *Eastern Daily Press*. "We used to feel pretty tired at the end of the day. Now everything is simple."

That boat continued in service until 1984 – a remarkable 60 years. If you're coming down the Yare by boat, you can still make her out, partially hidden in the reeds a few hundred yards upstream of the pub. Today the ferry continues to ply across the Yare dozens of times every day, charging £3.90 for cars and 50p for adults. The clank, clank, clank of the ferry chains echoes across the countryside as it has done for centuries.

'The clank, clank, clank of the ferry chains'.

PEOPLE – *David Archer*

Pub owner David Archer arrived at Reedham Ferry with his mother and father in 1949. After life in London, the 14-year-old was delighted to be living in the countryside, despite the basic facilities.

"The pub had no electricity and no water and the building was practically falling down," he told me.

"There wasn't that much call for the ferry then, so we spent a lot of our time sorting the house out. The pub was what they called a beer house – we only sold beer and cider. Country pubs didn't use to go for spirits then. We had plenty of land so we had a smallholding too. We kept pigs and chickens."

Sixty years later Mr Archer is still there. The pub now serves food and spirits as well as the beer his father's customers would recognise. The smallholding has been converted into a touring park for tents and caravans and the ferry continues to bring custom from the south bank. But can it continue in the twenty-first century?

David Archer.

"It's had its ups and downs over the years," he said.

"Takings did drop off considerably after the Norwich bypass opened in the early 1990s and I did wonder then if it was going to be able to pay for itself."

Stricter safety rules introduced after the *Marchioness* disaster on the River Thames in 1989, also made life difficult. But conversely as time goes on, the ferry's sheer uniqueness makes it more of an attraction. And when petrol prices leap up, Mr Archer quickly notices how drivers' behaviour changes accordingly.

"I've got a good team and my daughter Harriet is going to start working here full time too," he says. "We'll survive, we'll be fine."

Reedham's pubs

The Ship

Probably home to the Wherryman's Way's finest beer garden, The Ship is a perfect spot to watch the world go by. Hard up against Reedham Swing Bridge, it is also a good place to watch this grand old lady move back and forth with the river traffic. Inside too The Ship doesn't disappoint. Long-time landlord Graham Carlton has built up an impressive collection of photos chronicling the changing face of Reedham.

The Lord Nelson

The Lord Nelson was not purpose-built as a pub – unlike The Ship. Indeed one end was a garage until fifty or sixty years ago. In the late 1800s the landlord was James Hall of the famous Hall boatbuilding family. Present landlady Ros Carter – who took over with husband Bill in 2008 – says she has been told the building is home to no fewer than 12 ghosts.

Former pubs

The Railway Tavern closed in 2006 and was later converted into apartments. Located opposite the station, it was built when the railway arrived in the 1840s. Look out for the surviving pub sign if you are walking the Wherryman's Way circular walk.

The Ship.

The Lord Nelson.

The Eagle Tavern was on the corner of Station Road and Ferry Road – not far from The Railway Tavern. According to the norfolkpubs website, it closed in 1969. The building is now a private home called Eagle House.

The Brickmakers Arms was on Riverside opposite The Ship. The landlord here during much of the mid-1880s was Charles Hall, brother to James Hall, again of the boatbuilding family. It closed in 1914 and is now known as Rose Cottage.

Boatbuilding

Reedham will always have a special place in the annals of wherrydom because more were built here than anywhere else.

Much of the credit for that goes to the Hall family. According to Reedham's historian Sheila Hutchinson, James Hall set up a boatbuilding business here in the 1830s after moving from Norwich. His two sons James and Charles followed him into the trade, ending up with separate yards as well as running separate pubs – James at the Lord Nelson and Charles at the now defunct Brickmakers Arms.

Reedham; home of boatbuilders.

In those days a lot of Reedham employment would have been related to the river. Author TF Goodall paints a picture of the village in the late 1800s.

"With the first breath of spring, the boatyards and sheds become busy scenes. Masts and spars are scraped and varnished, blocks oiled, sails, ropes and rigging overhauled, spliced and mended."

Colin Sanderson.

Those busy scenes continue to this day. Brothers Colin and Steve Sanderson run separate yards on the same site used by first the Halls and then three generations of their own family.

"Some people still call it Hall's Yard," said Colin Sanderson, owner of the Sanderson Marine Craft hire boat company.

"Grandfather came here in the 1930s. He could see there was a future in hiring boats on the Broads. We were founder members of the Blakes co-operative when it started in the 1930s. It's no longer a co-operative but we still hire out boats with them now."

Throughout the 1960s his father Tony built his own boats here. The last to be built was the hire craft Sandstorm in 1990. Sandstorm thus followed down the slipway such illustrious names as *Maud, Dora, Fawn, Solace* and *Hathor*.

The Legend of Lodbrog

Lodbrog was a Danish prince who had the misfortune to be blown across the North Sea in a boat during a storm. The tempest blew him up the River Yare as far as Reedham, home to the court of King Edmund of East Anglia.

He was welcomed there but was later murdered by the King's huntsman, Bern, who had grown jealous of Lodbrog's popularity. Bern's punishment was to be put on a boat himself, without oars or sails. But he was blown back to Denmark where he told Lodbrog's sons that King Edmund had murdered Lodbrog.

The angry Danes assembled a mighty army and took to the seas to avenge this terrible injustice. They beat the Saxons and captured King Edmund, bringing an end to the Saxon dynasty in East Anglia. Edmund refused to renounce his Christian faith even after being tied to a tree and having arrows rained upon him.

He was later beheaded. Later his loyal followers found his body. Miraculously they also found his head some distance away being looked after by an uncharacteristically meek wolf.

His body was buried, with a small wooden chapel built to mark the spot. Later a grander church was built in a town which later became known as Bury St Edmunds.

Cupcakes

Annette St George was a young teenager when her parents took over the village grocery in Reedham in the mid-1960s. Little did she think then, that she would return to open a tearoom on the very same site more than 40 years later. Doris and Roy St George had moved up from Laindon in Essex. The shop was called Crouchen's Stores, the tourist trade was good and Annette never looked back.

"I thought I was in heaven. There were all these good-looking boys coming in off the boats. And after they left some of them would write to me with letters addressed to 'the dark-haired girl in the shop'. It was great."

While her parents moved on, Annette made a home in the village. She was a care worker in a residential home and later a day care assistant. By 2007, Crouchen's Stores was lying boarded up and unloved – depressing the rest of Reedham's Riverside in the process. Annette and husband Robert Terry took the plunge and bought the shop. Crouchen's Stores disappeared and on August 16th 2008, Cupcakes was born.

"When the sun is shining there are so many people who come to Reedham to enjoy these beautiful views," said Annette. "They walk here, they come by car, they come by boat, they come by train too. And we think a proper coffee and tea room is exactly what they want."

Annette Terry.

to the Waveney, then take this "New Cut" to the Yare and onto Norwich. What could possibly go wrong?

Ultimately, just about everything. Initially there were delays. The first Act of Parliament in 1826 was thrown out, thanks to opposition from Yarmouth, but a second in 1827 was successful. The Lowestoft end of the project went horribly over-budget, leaving the Norwich & Lowestoft Navigation Company to go cap in hand to a parliamentary group called the Exchequer Bill Loan Commissioners. They stumped up £50,000 allowing the New Cut to be built. The scheme was finally opened amid much fanfare in September 1833.

But within a year the project was in more financial trouble – and the Commissioners had to take over from the navigation company. To make matters worse, ships continued to go via Great Yarmouth. Eventually in 1842 the commissioners sold it on to six businessmen.

"They became the owners," said Peter Brown, "of a silting harbour protected by entrance works infested by the 'sea worm' and undermined by erosion, a virtually unused canal to Reedham and some works at Norwich. The investors in the company had lost over £80,000; the British Government had lost almost £50,000."

But fortunately those businessmen started talking to one of Victorian England's most dynamic entrepreneurs – Samuel Morton Peto. Almost single-handedly, Peto rescued the canal and built modern Lowestoft in the process. Amazingly quickly, he built the town's modern harbour, a rail link alongside the New Cut and the smart South Lowestoft buildings that established the town as a seaside resort.

The Norwich A Port campaign had descended into an expensive and bad-tempered row between Norwich and Yarmouth, in which neither side emerged with much credit. Perhaps it was fitting then, that the major beneficiary should be Lowestoft.

- The most recent threat to the New Cut's existence came with the floods of 1953. The following year the British Transport Commission sought an Act of Parliament to close it altogether, citing the cost of repairs as £100,000. This prompted much debate on the letters pages of the *Eastern Daily Press*. Some said it was a reasonable economy measure, others said closure would be "a blow at the heart of the whole system of waterways known so long and loved so much as The Broads." Thankfully the cost-cutters were fought off.

River scenes at Reedham during the race.

Heading through Reedham during the Yare Navigation Race

One Saturday every September the Yare Navigation Race changes the complexion of the River Yare. Dozens of cruiser class boats compete in a race from Coldham Hall Sailing Club to Breydon and back. These pictures were taken on the reaches between Reedham Ferry and Reedham during the 2006 race. For more information see Chapter 5.

This walk has two starting points depending on whether you live north or south of the river. Southerners start by crossing the River Yare at Reedham Ferry. Walk past the pub onto a road which strikes out away from the river across the marshes for a good half a mile. At the junction near the railway station head straight uphill onto a street called The Havaker, keeping the former Railway Tavern on your right. Turn right into Witton Green and follow the road to the end. Turn right onto a footpath and follow it along the edge of a field. At the road turn right and then immediately left at the war memorial down towards Riverside.

Northern walkers begin here on the Riverside. Walk the length of Reedham Quay and then turn left heading uphill on the Wherryman's Way proper. Turn right after the school into Holly Farm Road which soon crosses the railway line. This bridge also offers great views across the river and the marshes as well as the swing bridge.

After another half a mile the road takes a sharp left, leaving the Wherryman's Way proper to strike off straight ahead. We stick to the road. After a quarter of a mile, turn left onto one of two parallel footpaths just before a level crossing. The first follows the edge of the field, the second descends into a disused railway cutting before returning to the first path. You emerge back onto Holly Farm Road by the railway bridge.

From here retrace your steps to the war memorial. Turn left and look for a footpath on your left at the sharp right-hand bend. Head down the steps and follow the path down to the river bank. Southern walkers return to Reedham Ferry. Northern walkers need to turn right at the ferry to return to Reedham Riverside by road.

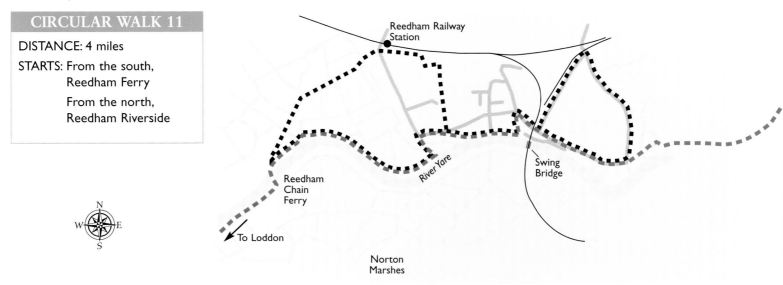

CIRCULAR WALK 11

DISTANCE: 4 miles

STARTS: From the south,
        Reedham Ferry

        From the north,
        Reedham Riverside

Reedham Railway Station

River Yare

Swing Bridge

Reedham Chain Ferry

To Loddon

Norton Marshes

Circular Walk 11: great views across the swing bridge.

THE WHERRYMAN'S WAY - DIRECTIONS

This chapter started with the short ferry ride across to the north bank of the Yare, courtesy of Reedham Ferry. Savour the moment. It is the only river crossing between Norwich's southern bypass and Great Yarmouth's Breydon Bridge. The Wherryman's Way would not be possible without it. After drinks at the Ferry Inn keep to the river, heading through a kissing gate near a converted windmill. The Yare winds right and then left leaving us with good views of riverside Reedham and the swing bridge.

Just as the view becomes clearer we are forced away from the river along a field-edge path which emerges onto a road. Turn right and take the right fork at the war memorial. Look out for the second memorial stone set into the grass as the road descends. This commemorates the 21 American servicemen killed in a mid-air collision between two B-17 bombers on February 21st 1944. The crash site – which lies to the north east of Reedham – was excavated by Channel 4's Time Team programme in 1998.

We pass Sandersons boatyard on our right before reaching the riverside. On a busy summer weekend this stretch is packed with tourists and day boats. Watching first-timers

In memory of the crew members of the
385th Bomb Group U.S. 8th A.F. B-17 bombers
Tragically killed in a collision over Reedham Marshes on the 21st February 1944

549th Bomb Squadron

1st Lt. Warren J. Pease
2nd Lt. Edward B. Brown
2nd Lt. Bernard Kaplan
2nd Lt. Robert E. Jenkins
Tech. Sgt. William R. Clift
Tech. Sgt. William Gill Jr.
Staff Sgt. Franklin C. Owsley
Staff Sgt. Junior M. Falls
Staff Sgt. Harold E. Dickason
Staff Sgt. Gail E. Bruner

550th Bomb Squadron

Capt. John N. Hutchison
2nd Lt. Charles G. Curtis
1st Lt. John E. Epps
1st Lt. Edmond J. Gamble
Tech. Sgt. Roy C. Kitner
Staff Sgt. Joseph J. Carpinetti
Tech. Sgt. William J. Dukes
Staff Sgt. John H. Erhardt
Staff Sgt. Emilio M. Corgnetti
Staff Sgt. Peter Bobulsky Jr.
Staff Sgt. Frank L. Creegan

Their name liveth for evermore

Remembering the B-17 bomber crews.

trying to moor their hire craft can be a good spectator sport. Keep on the quayside until you reach The Ship pub. Turn left heading uphill, with the pub on the right. The thatched building on the left used to be The Brickmakers Arms. It closed almost a century ago.

Turn right at the school into Holly Farm Road. This road crosses the Reedham to Lowestoft railway line, giving us great views of the swing bridge and the huge expanse of Norton Marshes beyond. Next, in the distance, look out for the dead-straight New Cut, connecting the Yare to the Waveney. A little further along, we pass Holly Farm Barn. This larch-clad building won a top award in 2006 for the "best one-off house designed by an architect in Britain." Eventually the road turns left but we continue straight on. The tower of St John the Baptist church looms on our left and you can start to make out the windmills that will form one of the highlights of Chapter 12.

Chapter 12 Breydon Water and the Berney Arms

"The hamlet of Berney Arms consists of two farmhouses, a row of small cottages, the remains of the old inn, and the tallest windmill in Norfolk. When January gales lash in over Breydon from the sea, when the marshes are spread deep with snow and the dykes are frozen hard, I know of no more bleak and desolate spot on the face of the earth."

Roy Clark, Black Sailed Traders, 1961

Now we really are out in the wilds. There are no villages left between here and Great Yarmouth. Just mile upon mile of winding Yare followed by mile upon mile of Breydon Water. Passing as much as a brick shed becomes an event along this bleak but beguiling stretch.

To our left are the empty spaces of Halvergate Marshes – the scene of an epic environmental battle in the 1980s. More on that later. Many centuries earlier, all of this area would have been underwater, part of a giant estuary of which Breydon is a surviving remnant.

Remember that on the south side of the river you are looking across to an island. The Yare and the Waveney form two sides of a triangle; the New Cut forms its base. With the exception of the odd farmhouse, the only buildings are – or were – dedicated to keeping the marshes drained. One of the highlights of this chapter is the unique collection of pumping devices around Polkey's Mill.

From there it is off to the Berney Arms hamlet. Somehow a pub and a station have survived here alongside the 70-foot high windmill – the tallest on the Broads. And finally we reach Breydon Water, whereupon the wildlife gets even wilder and more plentiful. Wading birds flock to the vast acres of inter-tidal mud. What this stretch lacks in people and buildings, it makes up for in everything else.

The Reedham Marshes Mills

As we've made our way downstream we've had glimpses of how the Yare Valley marshes have been drained over the years. But now in the most unlikely of places we get a set of buildings which comprise a complete history of Broads drainage mills. If they were more accessible they would surely be a major tourist attraction.

So, with thanks to Alison Yardy and the Norfolk Windmills Trust which has published a booklet on the subject, in chronological order of being built they are:

Polkey's Mill

Some sort of mill was here in the 1790s. It was probably hained (in other words heightened) about a hundred years later to enable it to take the patent sails. (Patent sails were invented by the Norfolk engineer William Cubitt in 1807. They allowed marshmen to adjust the sails on the turn, rather than having to stop the mill and adjust each one manually.) Polkey's probably drained the marshes until the early 1940s.

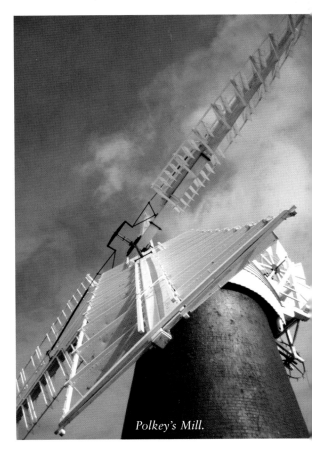

Polkey's Mill.

Opposite: The Yare snakes towards Breydon Water from the left, while the Waveney does the same on the right. The New Cut at the bottom of the picture completes Haddiscoe Island.

North Mill

Situated an unusually long way from the river, this shell of a mill dates back to about 1830. Notice how much smaller it is compared to the later mills. Last used about 1900.

Cadge's Mill

Built about 1870 or 1880 on the site of another mill and again kept going until roughly the 1940s. It fell derelict but was made weather-tight in the 1980s. Now houses the switchgear for the modern electric pump.

The Steam Engine House

Built in 1880 to house a single cylinder horizontal engine, powered by steam from a coal-fired boiler. This was not built to replace Polkey's Mill; rather to provide power when there was no wind.

The Diesel Engine Pumping Station

This is still home to two diesel engines which were installed in 1940 to take over from the combined efforts of wind and steam power. This building was moved as part of flood defence work in 2003. It could easily have been demolished, but survived to remind us of an unglamorous link in the historical chain. It carried on working till 1984.

North Mill.

Cadge's Mill.

The Electric Pump

Less obvious to the modern eye and yet more powerful than all the previous equipment put together. The gear kicks in automatically when dyke levels get higher. The most obvious element is the huge robotic arm which prevents the dyke getting blocked.

Steam engine pumping house.

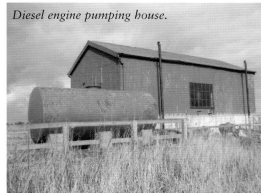
Diesel engine pumping house.

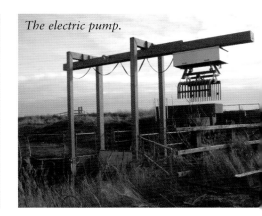
The electric pump.

The Battle of Halvergate Marshes

For centuries much of the land lying between Reedham and Great Yarmouth has been grazing marshes. Cattle were driven here from as far away as Scotland to enjoy the rich pasture. None other than Daniel Defoe talked of 40,000 "Scots cattle" coming every year to be fattened up "and most of them in the said marshes between Norwich, Beccles and Yarmouth".

Truth be told, the land was not good for anything else. It was so wet as to make arable farming completely impracticable. And the lack of roads combined with the profusion of dykes, made access difficult too.

But first diesel and then electric pumps became so powerful that suddenly a farmer could start to plant crops rather than fatten cattle. True, it required huge subsidies from Europe to make if profitable, but they almost seemed like a farmer's birthright at the time. Conversely, livestock farming was becoming unprofitable. The playing field was far from level and one by one farmers started to convert, irrevocably changing the landscape as they did so.

In his book on this subject Martin Ewans describes how important grazing was to the character of the marshes. You could only maintain what he calls the "botanical quality" of the dykes with a high water level. Without the embankments and the drainage systems "there would be extensive flooding and a reversion to reed-beds and lagoons".

Conservation groups were becoming concerned and a long and complicated row duly erupted in the early 1980s. From Friends of the Earth demos in front of dyke-digging machinery, to debates on the floor of the House of Commons, the row split the country.

Ultimately the environmental groups won. After several years of compromise and consultation, Halvergate became an "Environmentally Sensitive Area" where farmers would be paid a subsidy to maintain the landscape.

Writer Mark Cocker said the row revealed "the corrosive, tsunami-like destructive power of excessive grain subsidies flowing from the Common Agricultural Policy". Creating ESAs seemed controversial at the time. A generation later it seems no more than common sense. But the unchanging landscape to the north and west of Breydon Water had to be fought for, and was very nearly lost.

PEOPLE – *Andrew Lees*

Andrew Lees played a key role in the Battle of Halvergate Marshes. Born in Great Yarmouth in 1949, he was a keen environmental campaigner who had cut his teeth in Wales, preventing the authorities turning a rare wildlife habitat into a rubbish tip. Crymlyn Bog was subsequently designated a Site of Special Scientific Interest.

Returning to Norfolk, he set up Broadland Friends of the Earth to campaign against the plans to convert Halvergate Marshes. After a career with the Friends of the Earth nationally, he died in Madagascar in 1994 aged 46. He had been campaigning against plans to mine part of the island for titanium dioxide.

A small plaque has been dedicated to his memory outside Wickhampton Church, overlooking the Halvergate marshes.

In its obituary, *The Independent* newspaper said he brought " a messianic ardour" to his campaigning.

Andrew Lees's memorial outside Wickhampton Church.

"Just as the media was falling in love with the headlines which greenery and scare stories could generate, he displayed a fascination with hard data and a professionalism which kept him free of the charge of sensationalism. It is unlikely that anyone quite so naturally combative, but also innocently so, will be required or produced."

Berney Marshes Nature Reserve

If the Battle of Halvergate was all about draining the marshes, the RSPB's motto here is "keep it wet".

The charity bought its first stretch of land here in the aftermath of that controversy and now owns 1200 acres. In simple terms the three staff have to do two things: manage the water levels and keep the land grazed. The careful work of wardens Jim Rowe and Ralph Laughlin means breeding lapwing and redshank flock here in their thousands, together with many other species, notably wigeon and pink-footed geese.

"A site becomes of international importance when you get to the 20,000 bird mark," says site manager Mark Smart. "This site regularly reaches 80,000 or 90,000."

Unusually for an RSPB site manager, Mark's background is farming, no doubt helping him to work closely with the farmers who bring their cattle to graze here. The grazing season usually lasts from April through to mid-November. This reserve can handle 700 head of cattle, a mixture of cows with calves and beef animals.

The Berney Arms windmill before restoration.

"I can genuinely say that I can't think of another job I would rather be doing," he says.

"It's the sheer potential of the place. All the time we are finding new techniques where farmers and conservationists can work together. In effect we are farming here too. It's just that we have a slightly different crop; we're judged not by our yield, but by the number of chicks that fledge."

The tallest windmill on the Broads.

Berney Arms Mill

Berney Arms Mill stands seventy feet tall – a lonely giant in this flat landscape. Unusually for these parts, it was not built as a drainage mill. Instead it was used to grind cement. Indeed to truly understand it, you have to imagine it as the centrepiece of a busy cement works, surrounded by stationary steam engines and warehouses. The raw materials were chalk – delivered by wherry from Whitlingham – and clay – some of which was dredged from Breydon Water.

Author Sheila Hutchinson tracked down a newspaper advertisement from 1828 which describes the full extent of "Reedham Cement Works" with circular saws, tile kilns and brick sheds, cottages for workmen and "an unlimited supply of fine Brick and Tile earths upon the premises".

The mill itself is of a later vintage – somewhere between 1865 and 1870. Its grinding days came to an end in the 1880s after which it was converted to drainage work. Unusually the scoop wheel is some distance from the mill itself. The two are connected by a pinion.

This grand old girl of the Broads carried on until after the Second World War. She is the tallest mill on the Broads and according to author Luke Bonwick, her sails are the longest in the country.

The building is now owned by English Heritage which finished its restoration work in October 2007. The mill is not often open. Check English Heritage's website for more details.

PEOPLE – *Sheila Hutchinson*

Sheila Hutchinson is one of the few remaining people who can say they truly come from Berney Arms.

Yes, a farmhouse, a pub, a windmill and a railway halt, all somehow survive in this most isolated of locations. But when Sheila was a girl, there were houses, station cottages and a post office too: a proper hamlet with a definite sense of identity and community. Sheila grew up in what was called "No 1 Cottages", living there between 1947 and 1959. When No 1 was condemned, her family moved to No 7, until that too was knocked down in 1963.

"There was no running water and we had no electricity," she told me.

"We drank rainwater off the roof and do you know what we used for a filter? An old sock. In the winter you had to get a fire going in the fire grate to start with. Then you had to break the ice on a bucket of water, fill the kettle and put it on the fire. And that was just to get a wash."

Sheila Hutchinson.

Those days and those buildings are long gone. But Sheila and her husband Paul have dedicated much of the last ten years to painstakingly piecing together the lives of the other people who lived here. They have also written about the neighbouring communities like Reedham, Burgh Castle, Haddiscoe Island and – most recently – along the lower reaches of the River Bure.

All told, they have published eight books; each one packed full of historical data, census records, photos and memories. Paul specialises in the records; Sheila loves to talk to local people.

The books form an invaluable historical record, but Sheila rejects any notion of herself as a historian.

"All I know is that I was born and bred out in the marshes. I know the people down there and I know they'll talk to me. I like talking to the older people, we have a yarn together. I love to chat about the old days – and I love to see the look on their faces when they talk about the old days too."

Her first book "Berney Arms Past and Present" was published in 2000. To her surprise, all 500 copies sold out in just four weeks. Berney Arms might have been tiny, but it seemed as though everyone who had ever been there, wanted to know more.

"I go back there a few times a year," she said.

"It's really weird, you still feel like you're going home, but of course the buildings aren't there."

But thanks to the Hutchinsons, the memories most definitely are.

Berney Arms pub

Famously isolated, the Berney Arms is the pub the public cannot get to by road. By foot, by boat and by rail yes, but not by car. Former factory worker Tracy Bold and her electrician partner John Ralph moved here from Birmingham in 2007. They live there throughout the year and open the pub between mid-March and mid-November.

"In the winter it can be desolate and cold," said Tracy.

"It was a bit of a culture shock at first, you miss the silly little things like having the rubbish collected or being able to get a take-away. But it's a lovely spot and we absolutely adore the pub. It's a real old pub, with a lot of character to it."

The building now boasts a café and a shop as well as the pub itself. There is electricity, but no gas and water comes from a bore hole and a well. But why was the pub built here in the first place? Author Roy Clark posed the same question in his book *Black Sailed Traders*:

"You may wonder if an innkeeper ever made ends meet in such a place and why indeed an inn was ever built here. The answer is to be found in the fine towering windmill whose tarred brickwork and white painted sails rise impressively out of the flat marshland, dominating the whole scene around."

… With the mill and accompanying cement works came cottages and workers, all keen on a drink at the end of the day. Wherrymen too were glad of a safe haven before or after crossing Breydon Water. Today tourists need much the same. Most people arrive by boat, but there is also steady traffic from the tiny Berney Arms railway station across the marshes. Wherryman's Way walkers do their bit too. So, to ask Clark's question again, can an innkeeper still make ends meet?

"We love it here," says Tracy Bold; "We'll never be rich, but as long as we cover the bills we'll be OK."

Below left: The Berney Arms.

Below right: Tracy Bold and John Ralph.

A wherry on Breydon.

Breydon Water

Breydon Water feels as if it has its own habitat, its own micro-climate, its own loneliness. Our riverside walk is no longer; this is now a tidal estuary.

Two thousand years ago it was larger still. The sandbank which Great Yarmouth is built on had yet to develop; modern day Caister existed on one island while to the south Burgh Castle was on another. A bolder Breydon stretched inland as far as Reedham and up towards modern-day Potter Heigham and Horning. Today it remains the point where the three great Broads rivers become one. The Yare joins the Waveney at one end; the Bure adds its contribution at the other.

For hire cruisers all this can be a bit daunting – especially as Breydon is the only way to cross between the northern and southern Broads. Boats risk running aground unless they stay in the central channel – well marked by posts on either side.

Tide timetables suddenly become imperative. You need to get to Great Yarmouth at the right time.

Breydon's main claim to fame however, is its wildlife. It attracts waders and wildfowl by the thousand. In the past it attracted a particular breed of professional wildfowler too – well documented by Breydon's indefatigable naturalist Arthur Patterson. Today most of the estuary falls under the protective arm of the RSPB. Bleak? Usually. Exposed? Definitely. But by Norfolk's standards undoubtedly grand in scale. All in all, Breydon Water provides a suitably epic conclusion to the Wherryman's Way.

Breydon – where three ways meet

As well as the Wherryman's Way, two other long-distance paths run alongside Breydon Water.

The Angles Way runs for 77 miles from Great Yarmouth to Knettishall Heath near Thetford. Here it links up with yet another long-distance path, the Peddars Way which follows the route of an ancient Roman road to the North Norfolk coast.

Angles Way walkers follow the southern bank of Breydon Water to Burgh Castle, before heading south towards Belton, Fritton and Somerleyton. It does stray from the Waveney north of Oulton Broad before becoming a genuine valley walk further upriver.

The Weavers Way runs for 61 miles between Cromer and Great Yarmouth. It gets its name from the weaving industry which once flourished in the area. The walk starts on the pier at Cromer and passes through the National Trust estates at Felbrigg and Blickling. It then visits Aylsham and North Walsham, Stalham, Hickling and Potter Heigham. It hits the River Yare at Berney Arms and follows our route into Great Yarmouth.

ARCHIVE: *Arthur Patterson*

Breydon Water held "an unspeakable charm" to Arthur Patterson from the moment he first clapped eyes on it from his father's allotment on the outskirts of Great Yarmouth.

"I shall never forget," he wrote in his brilliant 1907 book *Wild Life on a Norfolk Estuary*, "my first sail across Breydon in the punt of a shoemaker friend, whose boat-shed today adjoins my own."

"Since those days of dreaming I have spent many pleasant hours upon and around this favourite haunt, in companionship with the birds that frequent it, and the rugged men who, from hard necessity as well as instinctive liking, have tried to wrest a precarious living out of its oozy depths."

Arthur Patterson – skipper of The Moorhen.

Patterson was desperately poor in an age when natural history was only practised by the very rich. But sheer force of personality meant he became a prolific writer, both of books and of newspaper articles under the pseudonym "John Knowlittle".

His houseboat Moorhen lay on the north bank of Breydon just past the half way point as we walk towards Yarmouth. Patterson describes it as being typical of the "Noah's Arks" used by smelters, eel fishers and wildfowlers.

"The hull, originally an old smack's boat, has been cabined over, a stove erected and stowage cupboards and settles added to suit the caprices or needs of the owners. In her palmier days the Moorhen drifted up and down the river and on to the Broads; but with age a boat gets leaky, and her skipper less restless. And Breydon grows on one so."

This is typical Patterson. Amidst his detailed knowledge of wildlife is a detailed love of life. Indeed a hundred years on, it is passages about the Breydon gunners like "Salt-fish" Jex, "Silky" Watson, "Pero" Pestell and "Pintail" Thomas that sing out to us as much as anything else.

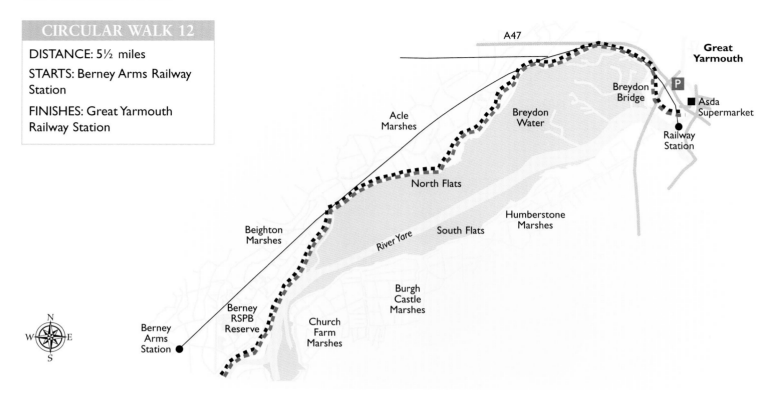

CIRCULAR WALK 12

DISTANCE: 5½ miles

STARTS: Berney Arms Railway Station

FINISHES: Great Yarmouth Railway Station

Circular Walk 12: Onto Breydon.

CIRCULAR WALK 12. This is a one-way walk which starts with a railway trip from Great Yarmouth to the tiny Berney Arms station. From the station take the path towards the Berney Arms Mill. From there, head to the river and follow the path towards the Berney Arms pub and Breydon beyond.

Follow the path all the way to Great Yarmouth passing under Breydon Bridge to emerge next to an Asda supermarket. Keep on the raised path and cross a road to return to the railway station.

THE WHERRYMAN'S WAY - DIRECTIONS

The directions at least are quite simple. Follow the river, then follow Breydon Water. In any case there are precious few alternatives.

From Reedham take the concrete track off Holly Farm Road heading parallel to the river. The tall tower of Reedham Church can be seen on the left, with the railway line to

Yarmouth bisecting the land in between. The minute you leave Reedham the landscape opens up. There is a lot to see and yet every single landmark looks isolated, such is the vastness of the vista. We will come to Polkey's Mill (with sails) and Cadge's Mill (without) first. They look too far to the left for the moment, but take this as a warning that our path will go in anything but a straight line. A tall boatshed at Burgh St Peter can be seen if you look across Haddiscoe Island; others further to the right belong to St Olaves.

Polkey's and Cadge's Mills lie next to Seven Mile House – the name a reference to its distance from Yarmouth. On a clear day at least you will now be able to see the very modern wind turbines at Scroby Sands off the coast. Look carefully from the highest point near Cadge's Mill and you should be able to spot at least 11 other windmills too.

Burgh Castle: substantial Roman walls. But we only see them from a distance on the Wherryman's Way.

From there it is another couple of miles to the beginning of Berney Marshes Nature Reserve, closely followed by Berney Arms Mill and Berney Arms pub. On the other side of the river, buildings are even rarer, one derelict stump of a windmill; another which has been capped and converted into a house. Look to the horizon just to the left of this conversion to see the tall walls of Burgh Castle. This Roman fort dates back to the third century AD.

Then Breydon looms large. Shiny mud flats ebb and flow with the tide, attracting vast hordes of wading birds – you can often see egrets. Solid wooden posts mark the only safe channel for boats crossing this inland estuary. It will feel colder and it's no surprise to learn that fog can arrive very suddenly. The weather forms a crucial part of the plot in Arthur Ransome's Broads classic Coot Club, when the Titmouse runs aground here.

It is five miles from the Berney Arms to Yarmouth. Five miles during which it is quite possible not to meet a soul. The occasional train will trundle through to our left; the buildings of Great Yarmouth gradually become more distinct on the right. Once again the only buildings are derelict windmills or electric pumps housed in anonymous brick sheds. The occasional set of stakes in the shallows show where houseboats once made their home. One – the Whimbrel – survived until 2008 until it fell victim to arsonists.

Last of the house boats: Whimbrel was destroyed by arsonists in 2008.

As civilization approaches, both road and railway squeeze in alongside our path. Just beyond the A47 lies the River Bure – the closest the Northern and Southern Broads come to each other. And then we reach Yarmouth. After isolation for so long, a busy town and Chapter 13 come as rather a shock.

Chapter 13 Great Yarmouth

"Leaving gay old Yarmouth behind with its ancient walls and turrets, its quaint rows, streets, curious houses, its hospitable inhabitants and pretty fisher-girls, we somewhat reluctantly proceed upon our way up the North River towards the heart of the Broad District."

Broadland Sport, Nicholas Everitt, 1902

Breydon Bridge was unveiled in 1985. It is on the site of an old railway bridge known as the Breydon Swing bridge which was demolished in 1962. Haven Bridge is in the foreground. There have been many bridges on this site, this one dates back to 1930.

Rather disappointingly, the ultimate destination of the Wherryman's Way is … Asda. Admittedly you can rest your feet at the wherry monument and the railway station could not be handier, but this is no place to end a walk. The town of Great Yarmouth is just across the River Bure and simply has to be explored. I will guide you through my own extension to the Wherryman's Way later in this chapter. Because Yarmouth is a fascinating town – or two towns in many respects. Much of modern Yarmouth faces the sea, making its living from the seaside and the tourists. The second – older – Yarmouth faces the river and this is where many of its grander buildings are to be found.

Daniel Defoe put it well: "The river lies on the west side of the town, and being grown very large and deep, by a conflux of all the rivers on this side [of] the county, forms the haven; and the town facing to the west also, and open to the river makes the finest quay in England, if not in Europe, not inferior even to that of Marseilles itself."

For almost a thousand years Yarmouth made its money from the herring industry. The season ran from roughly September to December. But, as historian Frank Meeres points out, herring were important all the year round because they could be preserved either by curing or smoking. The town's Time and Tide museum is on the site of one of the old smokehouses. Hundreds of boats and thousands of men caught tens of thousands of barrels of herrings, until the industry gradually declined in the 1950s and 1960s.

Geography dictates everything. There is very little space in that narrow strip of land between sea and river. So over the years a dense network of alleyways grew up running east-west. These were called rows and were too narrow for even a cart to get down. All but a handful were destroyed as part of a major rebuild after World War Two, but again, Time and Tide offers a good reconstruction.

Go to the other museums too. You don't expect them cheek by jowl with council flats, but Yarmouth's South Quay area specialises in interesting juxtapositions. The Nelson museum is particularly good. Whatever you do, don't let your tour of Yarmouth end at Asda.

The finishing line; the sculpture was unveiled in April 2009.

Asda: a disappointing final destination.

The Seven Havens of Yarmouth

The mouth of the River Yare has not always joined the sea between Great Yarmouth and Gorleston. In fact when Breydon Water was a much larger estuary, there were two outlets; one to the north near Caister called Grubb's Haven, the second to the south at Corton on the outskirts of modern Lowestoft. Both silted up. Indeed, the river has had seven different havens – or entrances – to the sea over the years. For centuries man battled with nature to keep the shifting sandbanks at bay.

Work on the seventh and final mouth started in the sixteenth century and crucially a Dutchman Joas Johnson was brought in as engineer. It was he who recommended the river's sharp left turn which survives to this day. In historian Frank Meeres's words, he created "a masterpiece of industrial engineering, which has endured for half a millennium, and he has probably had more effect on the landscape of Great Yarmouth than any other individual".

Arise Breydon Bridge.

PEOPLE – *Steve "Tug" Wilson*

If you walk the Wherryman's Way often enough you start to notice the distinctive red and yellow livery of The Southern Belle on the Yare's lower reaches. In the wheelhouse will be Steve "Tug" Wilson, originally a merchant seaman, now a skipper on inland waters. Several years ago Steve bought the Southern Belle with the idea of taking people out from Yarmouth across Breydon and beyond.

Steve "Tug" Wilson, skipper of the Southern Belle.

It was not a straightforward business. First the boat had to be completely restored, then there was the red tape. But now the Southern Belle has its regular berth just upstream from Haven Bridge and a steady stream of passengers are making the journey.

"It's by no means just the tourists," Steve told me as Breydon Bridge swung upwards to allow us to head upriver.

"The locals have really supported us too. A lot of people have lived here all their life and still never seen Breydon from the water."

The Southern Belle was built as a steam ferry boat in 1925. She was part of an estate owned by the Earl of Mount Edgcumbe and carried passengers between Cremyll and Plymouth on the Devon-Cornwall border. She has also been used by Plymouth dockyard and on the river Dart. In her latter years she fell on hard times; hence the restoration work by Steve and his son Colin.

On board you see Breydon in a completely new light. Wrecks of wherries loom out of the spray; traditional sailing cruisers heel dramatically in front of you. Then Steve's mate George has to stand on the prow pointing furiously as yet another tripper forgets the rules of the river before finally lurching to starboard.

Steve does more than just Breydon, there are also trips along the Waveney and occasional forays further up the Yare. In previous generations pleasure boats with names like *Pride of the Yare* and *Queen of the Broads* did exactly the same thing. Long may the tradition continue.

• For more information call Steve Wilson on 07906 020225

St Nicholas church

Many of England's smaller cathedrals have less of a sense of splendour about them, but St Nicholas remains a parish church, albeit the largest parish church in England.

It dates back to 1100 and is said to have been built by Bishop Herbert de Losinga, the man behind Norwich Cathedral. Under Oliver Cromwell the church was divided into three places of worship by brick walls within. A church guide says that the Presbyterians took the north aisle, the Independents the chancel while the Anglicans had the nave and the south aisle. Amazingly these walls were pulled down as late as the mid-nineteenth century.

Left: The 800th anniversary of the town's charter.

Middle: St Nicholas Church.

Right: One of several maritime gravestones.

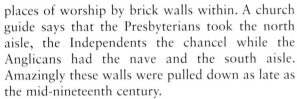

Having been restored by the Victorians it was then all but destroyed in 1942 by the Luftwaffe. Rebuilding work did not begin until 1957, with the church being reconsecrated in 1961.

Within the church, look out for St Andrew's chapel which, as the plaque, says "preserves the name of St Andrew's Church which stood on Fullers Hill from 1860 to 1961 and was built to serve the wherrymen who sailed on the neighbouring rivers".

Far left: St Nicholas after bomb damage.

139

ARCHIVE: *Yarmouth's Ferries*

Until relatively recently Yarmouth was home to two ferries across the Yare. The so-called Upper Ferry ran between South Quay and Southtown Road. It closed down in about 1954. Gorleston resident Margaret Dunnett remembers it well.

"I used it in the early 1950s to go and see my grandma," she told me.

"It was a small rowing boat and it used to cost one old penny. I can remember one of the ferrymen too, he was called Jumbo Wenn. I think it stopped, after they started running buses from Gorleston into Great Yarmouth."

The Lower Ferry in 1954: as a rowing boat.

The Lower Ferry survived for much longer. This service ran from Ferry Hill to South Denes Road. Steps running up from the river to Ye Olde Ferry Boat pub mark the spot on the Gorleston side. Current landlord Richard Burnett says it was well-used by workers at companies like Birds Eye and Erie Resistor.

"I've been told there was one shift at Birds Eye which started at 10pm. And the landlord at the time used to say he had just enough time to wash the glasses from the people going off to work before the ones finishing their shift came in. They say it used to be packed in here at that time."

Rowing boats were replaced by motor boats in 1954 and the service continued to thrive. A newspaper report in 1966 spoke of thousands happy to pay threepence to "save going round".

The Lower Ferry in 1954: as a motorboat.

The first signs of trouble in the archives come in 1974 when the weekend service had to be cut back because of a lack of demand. Only council subsidies kept it afloat during its latter years and the plug appears finally to have been pulled in 1997.

Views of Yarmouth

The patriotic Tudor Tavern.

At the seaside: Britannia Pier.

The 18th century Fisherman's Hospital: in effect almhouses.

Putford Protector at Southtown and left: The Pleasure Beach.

South Quay: as admired by Daniel Defoe.

Sunset over Breydon.

The town wall next to St Nicholas's churchyard.

The North West Tower, next to the River Bure.

Not always a tourist attraction.

THE WHERRYMAN'S WAY - DIRECTIONS

Officially the Wherryman's Way ends at the black-sailed monument between Asda and the railway station. But this ignores the rich history of the town beyond, which is why I suggest a two-mile extension.

Yarmouth's great secret is its amazing town walls – the most complete in the country. They were built in the 13th and 14th centuries and included several towers and gates, many of which survive. My Wherryman's Way finale simply follows their three sides, finishing with the watery fourth wall – the rivers Yare and Bure. So from the monument, ignore the pedestrian bridge and walk along the station access road. Cross the main road beyond onto a side street past the Suspension Bridge pub. This gives you a good view across the River Bure towards the North West tower – the start of the wall. The White Swan pub next to the tower used to be the haunt of wherrymen in times past.

From now on keep your eyes peeled. Remains of the wall will emerge and disappear several times. From the tower, cross another main road into Rampart Road. Then cross Northgate Street into Town Wall Road and keep right onto Ferrier Road for the first of the wall's magnificent stretches. Turn right into the graveyard of St Nicholas's Church. The hilly part of the churchyard shows the wall's original route. It re-emerges next to the Sainsbury supermarket car park. Cross Priory Plain and keep the wall to your right on Temple Road.

Turn right onto Market Gates and then left down a narrow alley with the walls on your left. Notice the tiny chunk of wall sandwiched between two shops as you emerge onto

Blackfriars Tower.

No need for gates today.

142

Haven Bridge: my finishing line.

…which still opens for river traffic.

The Time and Tide Musuem.

Regent Road. Turn left there and right at the crossroads into Alexandra Road, watching out for a tower behind the houses to your right.

At the end of Alexandra Road, turn right and then left onto Deneside at a complicated junction. Turn left onto St Peter's Road and then right onto Blackfriars Road, for another long stretch. Incidentally, The Recruit pub is a great example of a Yarmouth corner boozer along this section; the excellent Time and Tide museum and café is also very close.

Follow the wall as it starts to turn back to the river, using Mariners Road to get to South Quay. The wall used to extend to the water's edge. Purists might want to turn left and follow the Yare to its very mouth – still some two miles downriver. The rest of us will turn right towards Hall Quay passing many of Great Yarmouth's grandest buildings.

For me the Wherryman's Way ends in the middle of Haven Bridge, crossing the Yare at its mightiest. Look upstream for a glimpse of Breydon Water; look downstream to admire how Yarmouth still makes a living from its riverbank position. Then take a look at the thatched building on the far side of the river. This is a former icehouse, a relic of the days when ice from the frozen Broads was brought downstream to Yarmouth to help preserve fish. Check out the wherry weather vane on its roof and head for home.

The Recruit: flying the flag for old fashioned boozers.

…as it has done for decades.

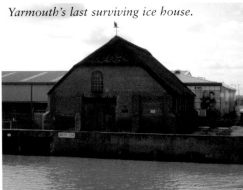

Yarmouth's last surviving ice house.

AND FINALLY...

If you have photos, memories or stories connected to the *Wherryman's Way* you can email Steve Silk at steveanddebbie.silk@virgin.net or contact him via his blog wherrymansweb.blogspot.com

Bibliography

Roy Clark - *Black-sailed Traders*
Jamie Campbell - *Hamilton's Navigations*
Mark Cocker - *Crow Country*
George Christopher Davies - *Norfolk Broads and Rivers*
George Christopher Davies - *The Swan and her Crew*
William Dutt - *The Norfolk Broads*
P H Emerson - *On English Lagoons*
Ted Ellis - *The Broads*
Nicholas Everitt - *Broadland Sport*
Martin Kirby - *Albion*
Robert Malster - *The Norfolk and Suffolk Broads*
Robert Malster - *Wherries and Wherrymen*
Arthur Patterson - *Wildfowlers and Poachers*
Mike Page - *A Broads Eye View*
Eugene Stone - *Ted Ellis, the People's Naturalist*
Ernest R Suffling - *The Land of the Broads*
James Wentworth Day - *Broadland Adventure*
James Wentworth Day - *Marshland Adventure*
Tessa West - *The Reed Flute*

Local History

Christopher Barringer - *Norwich in the 19th century*
The Bramerton Group - *Eleven Churches*
The Bramerton Society - *Bramerton*
Anne Cubitt and others - *Claxton A thousand years of history*
The Rev Kit Chalcroft and others - *Rockland St Mary*
Christina Crease & Carol Carpenter - *Loddon A Guided Historical Walk*
Christina Crease & Carol Carpenter – *The Before Your Time series*
S C Carpenter - *Langley with Hardley*
Mary Agnes Davey - *Hard Up Street*
Becky Ellis - *Carleton St Peter, A survey at 2000*
Jane Flatt - *Trowse This is Your Village*
Eunice Gladden - *The Premonstratensian Abbey of Langley Norfolk*
A A C Hedges - *Yarmouth is an Ancient Town*

Sheila Hutchinson - *Reedham Remembered*
Sheila Hutchinson - *Berney Arms Past and Present*
Clive King – *The Trowse Triangle*
Frank Meeres – *Great Yarmouth*
Trevor Nuthall - *Thorpe St Andrew*
Jack Points - *Surlingham A South Rivers Village*
William Rathbone Supple - *A History of Thorpe next Norwich*
Mary Rodgers - *The Rivers and Staithes of Tudor Norwich*
Colin Tooke - *Southtown and Gorleston*

Specialist Books

Martin Ewans - *The Battle for the Broads*
Martin George - *The Land Use, Ecology and Conservation of Broadland*
William Marshall - *The Rural Economy of Norfolk*
W A Money - *Crown Point Estate*
Brian Moss - *The Broads*
Nikolaus Pevsner and Bill Wilson – *Both Norfolk volumes of Pevsner Buildings of England*
Jack Points - *Chain Ferries over the Yare*
Ebenezer Walter Priest - *Norfolk Rivers and Streams*
Beryl Tooley - *Scribblings of a Yarmouth Naturalist*
Percy Watts - *467th Bombardment Group (H) in World War Two*
Tom Williamson - *Norfolk Broads: a landscape history*
Alison Yardy - *Mills of the Halvergate Marshes*

Articles and Papers

JRL Allen, EJ Rose and MG Fulford – *Re-use of Roman Stone in the Reedham Area of East Norfolk*
Peter Brown - *The Norwich and Lowestoft Navigation: Why did it fail?*
Barbara Cornford - *The Sea Breach Commissioners in East Norfolk*
Alan Davison - *The Evolution of Settlement in Three Parishes in SE Norfolk (East Anglian*

Archaeology)
Chris Fisher - *Early Chalk Tramways at Whitlingham (Norfolk Industrial Archaeology Society)*
Chris Fisher - *Farmer Pyke's Forgotten Railway (NIAS)*
EDP - *various articles and letters on Billy Bluelight, Surlingham Ferry, The New Cut and The Lower Ferry, Gt Yarmouth*
Geoffrey Kelly - *The Ferry House Surlingham*
Cecil Nicholls - *Along the banks of the River Chet in the 1930s and 1940s*
Norwich City Council - *Trowse Millgate Conservation Area Appraisal*
Theole EB Douglas Sherwood - *The Norfolk Keel (thesis)*
Owen Thompson - *Newton Hall, Trowse Newton*
Anthony Ward - *Smoke Drifting over the Reeds (NIAS)*
Dr Thomas C Welsh - *Report of a Survey of the Vicinity of Claxton Castle*
James Wentworth Day - *Wherries and Wherrymen (Country Life)*
James Wentworth Day - *The King of Rockland Broad (Country Life)*
James Wentworth Day - *The Last of the Norfolk Horse Ferries (Country Life)*
James Wentworth Day - *In a Lonely Land (Country Life)*

Maps

Bryant's Map of Norfolk in 1826
OS 1st edition – Cassini Historical Maps
OS Explorer OL40 The Broads

Websites

Andrewleestrust.org.uk
Berneyarms.co.uk
Heritage.norfolk.gov.uk
Norfolkchurches.co.uk
Norfolkmills.co.uk
Norfolkpubs.co.uk
Rocklandwa.co.uk